Hunting
North America's
Big Bear

Grizzly, Brown And Polar Bear
Hunting Techniques And Adventures

Hunting North America's Big Bear

Grizzly, Brown And Polar Bear
Hunting Techniques And Adventures

Hunter's Information Series™
North American Hunting Club
Minneapolis, Minnesota

Hunting North America's Big Bear
Grizzly, Brown And Polar Bear
Hunting Techniques And Adventures

Copyright© 1989, J. Wayne Fears

Library of Congress Catalog Card Number 89-60285
ISBN 0-914697-20-X

Printed in U.S.A.
        5   6   7   8   9

Contents

Acknowledgments

Hunting North America's Big Bear is a comprehensive, common-sense book about hunting this continent's most dangerous game. The author has included exciting big bear hunting adventures from North America's rugged frontiersmen, and recommendations from today's guides and outfitters who earn their living by chasing grizzly, brown and polar bear in North America's most desolate country.

For their behind the scenes work, special thanks to: NAHC Publisher Mark LaBarbera, Editor Bill Miller, Associate Editor Dan Dietrich, Editorial Assistants Karyl Dodge and Deb Morem, Member Products Manager Mike Vail and Special Projects Coordinator Linda Kalinowski.

Steven F. Burke, President
North American Hunting Club

Photo Credits

In addition to examples of his own talent, the author has included photographs from: Fred Bear, Dennis Campbell, Judd Cooney, Sherry K. Fears, Cy Ford, Bob Ford, David Hofius, Larry Kelly, Jerome Knap, Leonard Lee Rue III, Leonard Lee Rue, Jr., Mark Meekin, Lucky Nightingale, David O'Keefe, Tom Rigden and Barry Stewart. Product photos, in some instances, were supplied by the manufacturer.

About The Author

As the son of a trapper, J. Wayne Fears grew up hunting. He earned wildlife degrees from Auburn University and the University of Georgia. From 1964 to 1966 he was a wildlife specialist with the University of Georgia. Then in 1966 he started guiding and outfitting big game hunters. From 1974 to 1982, Fears was the head of the Forest Recreation division of a large pulp and paper corporation. As a part of this job, he set up and personally directed several hunting operations in Alaska, British Columbia, Colorado and Alabama.

In 1982, Fears left the pulp and paper corporation to develop his own guiding and outfitting business which consisted of three hunting lodges. He and his wife, Sherry, operated these lodges for four years. In 1986, they sold this business to devote their time to outdoor writing and wildlife management consulting.

Today, Fears is a full-time outdoor writer with over 2,500 magazine articles and 14 books to his credit. He is the outdoor editor of *The Anniston Star* newspaper in Alabama. He is a recognized authority on shooting subjects and the hunting/outdoor equipment editor at both *Shooting Times* and *Handgun Quarterly* magazines and a contributing editor to *North American Hunter* and *Bowhunting World* magazines.

He is a past president of the Southeastern Outdoor Press Association and the Georgia Outdoor Writers Association. Fears

has served on the board of directors of the Outdoor Writers Association of America and has won numerous national writing awards.

Due to his work in the Arctic, Fears was elected to membership in the Explorers Club and is a founding member and director of the Longhunter Society. He has served on the board of directors of Safari Club International and is past president of the Alabama chapter.

He and Sherry, who is also an outdoor writer, reside in Heflin, Alabama. They have their own wildlife management and shooting research area surrounded by a national forest.

Fears' fascination with big bear began with his first grizzly hunt on which he took a bear with one shot. His next grizzly took five shots and almost got into his hip pocket. He considers big bear to be North America's most exciting big game animals and is an active supporter of bear management.

It is his belief that big bear play an important role in the hunter's world. The mystique, power and unpredictability of these massive animals gives most hunters a desire to enter truly wild country and to test themselves against an animal that can, in turn, hunt and destroy the hunter. Fears believes we need these impressive creatures to fill out the adventure of hunting in North America and that the Far North would not be the same without them.

With this strong feeling about North America's bear, Fears calls upon his own experiences, those who guide bear hunters and wildlife biologists to put together this book. This NAHC Hunter's Information Series™ book will show you how to plan and execute your own bear hunt and it will entertain you with actual stories about big bear hunting.

Dedication

To Brooke, Brandi and Justin. May there be huntable populations of big bear when your time comes.

1

Hunting Big Bear:
What Makes It So Special?

Harvey Cardinal was more than the average hunter. He was an Indian who had spent his life trapping, hunting and guiding hunters in northeastern British Columbia. Having grown up in grizzly country, he knew the big bear were unpredictable and smart.

On a fateful day in January, 1970, there were 10 inches of snow on the ground. Nighttime temperatures were as low as 30 degrees below zero when Cardinal left his home near Fort St. John to visit some friends who were trapping along the Doig River in British Columbia.

Cardinal arrived at his friends' cabin amid a lot of excitement. The trappers had come across fresh tracks of a large grizzly that morning as they ran their trapline. It wasn't unusual to see a grizzly, as there were many of them in the area, but it was odd that the bear was not hibernating during this mid-winter, bitter cold.

While it struck Cardinal as odd that the bear would be out of its den in this extreme cold, he couldn't resist thinking about the money he could get for a grizzly pelt with a winter coat. The prospect of extra cash stuck with him that night. At daybreak he left the cabin with his rifle. He was off to hunt the bear alone.

As he set out across the snow-covered ground, he probably gave some thought to how dangerous a grizzly can be. There had been, over the years, three grizzly attacks in that area.

Two attacks involved hunting guides, one who jumped off a cliff to save his life and another who was charged by a wounded bear he was trailing for a hunter. The third victim was a hunter who was mauled when he walked up on a moose kill that a grizzly was guarding.

Cardinal reached the bear tracks the trappers had found and started following them. As he stayed on the trail, the tracks became fresher, and with his experience, he must have known that he was getting close to the bear. Without warning, a massive paw struck the side of Cardinal's head from behind, shattering his skull. The bear had evidently hidden in ambush and allowed Cardinal to walk by so that it could attack from the rear. Its attack was obviously without warning, as Cardinal's mittens were still on his hands. His rifle's safety was still on.

When Cardinal didn't return, a search party was organized early the next morning. They soon found a horrifying sight. Much of Cardinal's upper body had been eaten by the bear.

Welcome to the exciting world of big bear hunting! It is a world that is full of adventure where mistakes can be deadly.

Most big game hunters name the grizzly, brown or polar bear as the North American game animal they would most like to hunt. Those who have never hunted big bear often want one because of magazine articles they've read about the close calls encountered when hunting these animals. Another reason many hunters want to take one of the big bear is because a big bear is a massive and impressive trophy in anyone's home or office.

For those who have hunted these giant carnivores, the reasons for feeling compelled to chase them is far deeper than what is found in a magazine story or a rug. It is the respect and admiration for a creature that almost defies description. What you can say about one bear won't apply to another bear. What a bear will do today, he won't tomorrow. When you think he's dumb, he will make you a fool. When you think he's smart, he will surprise you with a less-than-smart act. In short, they are the most unpredictable animals we hunt in North America.

When you add to that the fact that they are intelligent, vindictive, courageous, cunning, stubborn, shy, tenacious, strong, dangerous and found in some of the most beautiful yet harsh country in the world, you have everything a hunter could want in a trophy animal.

It is the danger associated with hunting big bear that gets more attention from hunters than anything else, and perhaps rightfully

NAHC member Bill Brooks with his 9-foot, 3-inch grizzly taken in Alaska with guide Bob Hannon. For his successful hunt, Bill received the 1986 NAHC President's Trophy.

so. Under the right conditions, they will hunt you just as hard as you hunt them. As I researched this book, I tried to determine a reasonably accurate number of bear attacks during the past 50 years by polar, grizzly and brown bear. What I learned is that it is not possible. There is no single record-keeping source for such incidences, and there have undoubtedly been many unrecorded maulings and close calls.

Almost everyone who guides or outfits hunters for these big bear has had some close calls. Guy Anttila of Taku Safari, Inc., a guiding service in British Columbia, told me the most aggressive behavior he had ever seen displayed by a grizzly occurred in October, 1986. He and his wife were photographing grizzlies that were trying to catch salmon on the Taku River. The Anttilas had just completed their fall hunting season and were taking a break by filming bear.

It was their second day of filming, and they had recorded some good footage of several grizzlies. Now they were concentrating their efforts on a sow with a three-year-old cub still traveling with her. After an hour of chasing and eating salmon, the sow and cub crossed over to the side of the river where the Anttilas were hidden in some driftwood. Unaware of the humans' presence, the sow and cub walked into the willows and alders some 80 yards away. The Anttilas knew the sow would soon pick up their scent, as the wind was blowing toward her.

Guy assumed the sow and cub would leave the area once they picked up their scent. With their rifle leaning against the drift logs, the Anttilas discussed their photography. That's when things got interesting. Luckily, Guy was facing the right direction to see the big sow break out of the willows at a distance of 45 yards. She was coming on the run, up the scent trail, her head down in a silent charge. Sand was flying behind every step.

Anttila shouted at the bear as he reached for the rifle, but this just gave the bear a better fix on their location. The next thing Anttila knew, the open sights on his .375 H&H Magnum were centered on the bear. He instinctively shifted the aim slightly to the right to miss the face as he fired.

The bullet hit the sow in the left shoulder, stopping her.

The charge lasted only about four seconds. The sow tried to get up, but her left leg kept buckling under her. This infuriated the bear, now roaring and making all the sounds of a charging bear. A second shot through the shoulder killed her.

A similar charge happened to a guide in British Columbia, North American Hunting Club Life Member Igor Steciw. In 1979 he was guiding a hunter for moose and black bear. It was October, and the day had been cloudy with intermittent rain. Late in the afternoon, the weather cleared and Steciw thought it would be a good time to sit on a hillside and do some glassing. They were near a small, unnamed lake at the upper drainage of the Skeena River, and the coho salmon were at the height of their spawning run.

After only 15 minutes on the hillside, the two men heard the loud crack of a branch breaking, then another. When they looked toward the sound, they saw a large grizzly walking the shoreline of the lake about 300 yards away. Since the hunter didn't have a grizzly tag, they took pictures of the bear as he ambled in their direction. In the last frame Steciw took, the bear was about 25

Paul Burke, founder of the North American Hunting Club and NAHC Life Member #1, with his Boone & Crockett record book grizzly bear. The grizzly scored 24 1/16 B&C points, and was the largest taken in British Columbia during the 1978 season. Paul hunted with Love Bros. & Lee. A full-body mount of the bruin greets visitors at NAHC headquarters.

yards away and heard the camera shutter click. That got the bear excited. It barked a few times and stood on its hind legs. Steciw called out to the bear, "Go on home, boy," expecting it to take off in a run. But the bear grunted, went back down on all fours, and stood up again.

Again Igor yelled, "Go on, get out of here." To the two men's amazement, the bear now went down on all fours and charged at full speed, taking big leaps toward the hunters. Steciw's rifle went up to his shoulder in a flash, and he fired once, twice and a third time. The third shot turned back the charge. The bear was now sideways at about 20 feet. At this point, Steciw took aim behind the left shoulder and fired. The bear wavered through a few steps, went down and rolled off the hill. All was quiet again. The bear squared 7 feet 11 inches and was dark brown with silver tips from its forehead to the tail.

The unpredictable nature of large bear keeps a hunter on his toes all the time, whether he is in the field hunting or in camp resting. A good example of this was related to me by Jerome Knap of Canada North Outfitting, a polar bear guiding service. One of Jerome's hunters and an Eskimo guide were polar bear hunting at the northern end of Baffin Island at the mouth of Admiralty Inlet. During the first two days of the hunt, the hunter saw nine bear, including two males in the nine-foot class. Hunters don't normally pass up nine-foot bear, but in this case, the hunter did so because he and his guides had found some day-old tracks of a bear that would go over 11 feet. They decided to hold out for that bear.

On the third morning, the hunters were still asleep in an igloo when the chained dogs started to bark. One of the guides, thinking another dog team was approaching, crawled out of the igloo to see what was happening. There, just 15 yards from the igloo, was a nine-foot polar bear eating on a seal carcass that had been shot the day before for food. The guide retreated into the igloo and told the hunter.

Thinking it a good opportunity to photograph a polar bear, the hunter used his knife to chip a hole in the side of the igloo large enough to stick his camera lens through. As he started to take a picture, the bear looked up and saw the black spot on the side of the igloo. It charged instantly.

The igloo half collapsed under the bear's attack. Then, backing away, the bear spotted the men. As the bruin charged again, the hunter grabbed his rifle and shot, killing the bear two paces away.

While the brown and grizzly bear seem to dislike the scent of man, there are occasions when it doesn't seem to matter. One fall I was hunting caribou on the Alaskan Peninsula in an area of low-rolling tundra hills scattered with small lakes. There was little vegetation in the area, and long stalks were required to get near the caribou bulls found moving through the area. Walking across the wet tussocks was tough and time-consuming.

Early one morning, I spotted two large bulls about three miles from my small spike camp and set out to try for the larger of the two. By the time I got to where the bulls had been, they had moved on, putting too much distance between us to cover that day. Disappointed, I started the long walk back to camp.

As I topped the first hill on my return trip, I looked back to see a large brown bear following me some 400 yards back. He was a beautiful animal with long hair waving in the stiff breeze which blew from me to him. I didn't have a bear tag, so I just sat down to admire him and see what his plans were.

With the wind blowing toward him, he must have scented me, but it didn't seem to have any effect. When I sat down, he lay down. I waited and he waited. When I got up, he got up. Once again I headed back toward camp, now looking back more than ahead. When I would go down into a low area and couldn't see him, I would always be ready as I approached the top of the next hill, half expecting him to be in front of me.

However, he never closed the distance, and he basically did whatever I did. When I reached camp, he disappeared just as quickly as he had appeared, and I never saw him again. Not because I wasn't looking, though.

Most big bear are naturally shy, and if given the chance, would prefer to avoid a confrontation with man. But the polar bear doesn't see it that way. In fact, he has the reputation of being the only animal in the world that will instinctively stalk and kill a man. Jerome Knap points out that a polar bear doesn't have to be wounded to be dangerous, nor does it have to be disturbed or angered or have its young threatened. All you have to do is be in its kingdom of ice and snow. You are flesh, blood and bones, and thereby edible.

Knap tells me that every year, a dozen or more polar bear are killed in the Canadian Arctic because they attacked or were about to attack people. Polar bear stalk men whenever they are hungry, which is most of the time. Over the years that his company has been arranging polar bear hunts, a number of hunters filled their tags in camp. As Knap explains, ''Some of these hunters were not

Habitat for big bear is in North America's most beautiful, yet harsh, country. Ideal grizzly habitat is where the forest thins at higher elevations and around snow slides.

even fully dressed when the bear were shot. At first glance, this seems to be a rather anticlimactic way to shoot a polar bear, until you remember that the bear came to camp to feed on whatever was available, including the hunter.''

Another fact about the big bear that makes them special to the big game hunter is their tenacity. These animals have a desire to keep on living unmatched by any other animal. Not only that, but they are built to take a lot of punishment and stay on their feet. As will be illustrated throughout this book, the grizzly, brown and polar bear can take a lot of lead from hunters. If he is not anchored with broken shoulders, he can ''get in your hip pocket'' in a hurry or make it into the brush, which assures you of much more excitement. More excitement than many hunters are ready for!

I have seen a grizzly hit through the lungs stay on his feet and go for 2½ miles, leaving not a drop of blood for the first one-half mile, before he dropped dead. That was an exciting trailing job.

I once spent the night in a remote Indian village where one of the elder members invited me to his house to look at a huge grizzly rug he had. That rug had 21 holes in it where the bear had been hit. The old man told me that he and his family had ambushed the bear at the bottom of a cliff. Standing on the top of the cliff, they shot until the bear went down. The Indians were about out of ammo when the bear finally fell.

Jerome Knap tells of one of his hunters who had a close call with a wounded polar bear because the scope mounts on the hunter's rifle had jarred loose. As a result, the rifle was shooting a foot to the left at 100 yards. Before the hunter discovered this problem, he got an opportunity to take a big bear. He emptied his rifle at the bear, hitting it each time, but never with a shot that would break him down. The guide finally dropped the bear four feet from them. The bear took seven hits before he went down.

The Far North has many stories of bear that took several solid hits, yet managed to hunt the hunters or to ambush them. I was on one blood trail back in the 1970s with three other hunters following a mountain grizzly that had taken three shots in the upper part of the body. There was little blood to follow, and the grizzly had run into a wide creek bed covered with willows which stood about head high to a man. One of the banks of the creek was about 10 feet tall, and a hunter walking on it could see down into some of the willows. The other bank was low and almost 100 yards away, offering no help. A hunter from Minnesota climbed up on the high bank, and the other three of us, walking abreast about eight feet apart, began to pick our way through the tangle of willows. The bear had been in the willows for over an hour, and we all hoped he was now dead.

It was unusually warm as we ever-so-slowly moved a few feet, stopping often to listen for any sign of life up ahead.

It is always an uncomfortable feeling to follow a hit bear, and in the thick willows with insects swarming all around my head, it was almost smothering. I came to a ditch-like depression that I had to climb into, and as I slid down the bank, my .30-06 felt more like an air rifle. I peeked over the opposite bank before I climbed up and thought to myself, "How do I get myself into these situations?"

Moving back into the willows, I whistled to let the other two hunters know it was me. When I did, a brown mass exploded right in front of me. "God, it's 10 feet tall!" I thought, as I swung my rifle up.

"Damn, it's running over me!" I heard the hunter just to my left cry.

Big bear hunting can be extremely demanding—both physically and mentally. Physically, the terrain is rugged, the weather extreme and the country desolate. Mentally, it's demanding to know that under the right conditions, big bear will hunt you just as hard as you hunt them.

The crashing of willows was deafening, and this was all going on within a few feet of me. I couldn't identify enough of the creature to get a sight picture. My mind raced as I moved the rifle around. "You're in trouble, Fears, if you don't put this bear down fast," I told myself. Then on top of the brown mass I saw the white antlers of a bull moose. He had been bedded down in a small opening in the willows and was so confused with the three of us being in the willows with him that he almost ran over two of us. Why one of us didn't shoot him, I'll never know.

Soon after the moose scare was over, the hunter on the high bank shouted. He had spotted the bear dead at the bottom of the bank. I don't think I have ever been more glad to have a trailing session over. The moose had about sapped all the courage out of us.

There is no other hunt in North America that can give you the thrill of a big bear hunt.

Aside from the bear themselves, other things associated with bear hunting make it special. The hunt can include a long, leisurely morning spent sitting against a warm, sun-bathed rock using binoculars to cover every inch of a vast valley or opposite mountain slope. When a bear is spotted, it may suddenly mean a three-mile hike over boggy ground, through alder jungles and across cold, rushing streams. It may incorporate a climb up a slope that's so steep you wonder if you can get up it. This is typical of inland grizzly hunting.

On early spring hunts, you may be on snowshoes doing the same things. Most of the guides I've hunted and worked with will confirm this: Your chance of success on grizzlies is directly related to how good a shape you are in. The country is vast and rough, and bear are scattered, so cross-country travel on foot is a major part of the hunt.

Brown bear hunting can be different. My wife and I have hunted along the coast of British Columbia with guide Cy Ford where the day was divided between hours of cruising waterways in a large flatbottom boat, sitting and watching tidal flats and walking in hip boots through thick brush to get to openings along the creeks in that area. The air was often thundering with the sound of snow slides as the spring thaw occurred. Our camp was a small cabin cruiser, and we were ever mindful of the drastic changes in the tide.

Other brown bear hunts may involve floating small rivers and creeks with an inflatable boat. One of the best stories I've heard that describes how exciting this type of hunting can be is told by Bob Good, a well-known handgun hunter and outdoor writer from the Denver area. Good was hunting brown bear with guide Ken Fanning along a small creek near Yakutat, Alaska. Here is the story in Good's words:

"We were floating a small side stream of the Situk when we came to a narrow cut barely wide enough to float the raft. The banks were about three feet high over us, and covered with a mix of alder stands and bear grass. We had just got started into the cut when an underwater branch snagged the bottom of the raft, stopping our forward progress. We were swinging back and forth like a clock pendulum banging against tangles of roots on either side. I turned to look at Ken just in time to see his jaw hit his chest. In brown bear country, you don't have to ask what has caused your partner's sudden start.

"Spinning back around, I snatched the Contender from the holster and looked up. An eight-foot brown bear boar was standing directly over us, trying to understand what in the world had disturbed his stream-side nap. We were so close that I'm sure in his limited eyesight he was looking at the whole bobbing unit of raft and hunters as some two-headed monster about the size of an elephant that was gurgling an endless spray of white foam. He looked upset, but confused. This was not a bear we wanted to shoot. Number one, he wasn't quite trophy size, and number two, with one easy jump, even fatally wounded, he could land in our stuck craft faster than two panicked hunters could ever execute a satisfactory abandon-ship drill. It was a stand-off.

"Behind me, I heard the safety catch on Ken's .458 click ahead. I'd never been able to hear it before. At the moment, it seemed ominously loud. Ken was now talking in loud expletives to the bear, advising him it was in his best *&*! interest to vacate the area. The bear dropped to all fours, took two steps forward and reared erect again, this time popping his teeth rapidly—a bad sign. Only then did we notice the recently-ripped hide and dried blood on his face.

"This guy was apparently resting after a fight when we came merrily along and banged into his bedside. He was going to be long on anger and short on caution. It was not a good situation. 'Tense' doesn't quite describe it.

"At the bear's feet was a broken branch.

" 'Bob, if that son-of-a-b——h steps over that branch, unload

It is the danger associated with hunting big bear that gets much attention from hunters, and perhaps rightfully so. Big bear are the most unpredictable animals in North America.

on him with everything you've got, and don't stop shooting until you are empty!' Ken instructed.

"By now, I had the Contender zeroed on the bear's chest and the .44 Redhawk balanced in my lap for a quick grab. I had already decided that the broken branch was the demarcation line even before Ken spoke. The bear continued to stare at us with that piggish look bear have that sends a chill right through you. His jaws continued to snap and pop. The air was tense with electricity. As the raft swung and bobbed with the current, I tried to stay calm and keep the crosshairs pointed somewhere near the bear's brisket. Neither one was easy.

"With a 'woof,' the bear suddenly whirled and was gone, the swishing alders marking his retreat. Neither Ken nor I moved until we were certain the irritated bear was indeed gone.

"Slowly we returned the guns to rest position and looked at each other with sheepish grins. After unsnagging our raft, we floated on, trying to offset the seriousness of the previous predicament with a nervous chuckle, but we were unusually tense the rest of the day. That bear had been just too close.

"Two years later, Ken's very capable assistant guide, Pierce Nelson, and I killed a bear within 200 yards of that same cut."

Some brown bear hunting during the fall is done by watching streams filled with salmon. This might mean a 10-minute walk from a spike camp or a two-hour walk through boggy alders from a base camp. Other hunts may be from a boat glassing sandy beaches. Once the bear is spotted, a long and sometimes interesting stalk through dark timber may be in store before you can get into a good shooting position.

The polar bear hunt of today is done only one way: the traditional Eskimo hunt with dog team. It is a most demanding hunt, both physically and mentally. It involves going out on the polar ice, living there in igloos or tents with Eskimo guides and meeting the polar bear on his own terms.

Techniques vary from sitting on high icebergs and using binoculars for hours to finding fresh tracks and staying with them for three or four days, camping on the tracks at night.

The hunter will find the wind and temperatures bitter and the camps less than plush. The paying hunter will be expected to join in with his guides to help with camp chores. This hunt tests both the hunter and his equipment.

The weather that goes with bear hunting helps make it special and has been known to cause many hunters to stop their hunt early

Alaskan big bear guide Tom Rigden of Mountain Enterprises Guide Service with a brown bear that squared more than 10 feet. The Alaskan brown bear harvest continues at a healthy rate.

Bear hunting camps are always special. Some are small and uncomfortable, others large and homey. But all are memorable.

to retreat to the comforts of the modern world. Obviously, below-zero temperatures, wind and snow are typical in polar bear country. Grizzly and brown bear weather varies depending upon whether it is a spring or fall hunt and where you are hunting. I normally think of bear hunting weather as being cold with wind-blown rain and some snow. I have seen hunts that were in deep snow with more snow falling off and on for the entire hunt. I have hunted on days with a mixture of temperatures warm enough to bring out the insects by day, and a light snowfall at night. I have had a spike camp blown away and others so wet there wasn't a dry place to sleep. I have been snowed in a spike camp until the food almost ran out.

I loved every one of those camps.

While I have been on some relatively easy bear hunts, most were hard work with long hours spent in rough weather conditions. But that's part of what makes bear hunting special. Not everyone is cut out to hunt big bear. For those of you who are, hang on. This book is for you.

If your idea of fun is sitting on a gas can under a dripping tarp, eating soggy freeze-dried food after walking eight miles in a downpour, knowing that your wet sleeping bag is waiting for you and that tomorrow morning you will again try to get within 50 yards of one of the smartest, most dangerous animals on earth, then welcome to the world of big bear hunting.

2

Big Bear
Of North America

It was the proudest moment of Bill Dawson's life, the realization of a dream he had fostered since he was a little boy. As my hunting partner, Bill was exhausted after nine long days of hunting the roughest country he had ever seen in the most miserable weather he had ever experienced. He had never known fear the way it raced through his tired body just a few minutes earlier, as our guide had encouraged him to get within 50 yards of a nervous creature that weighed close to half a ton and had a reputation as a man-killer.

For nine days, Dawson, who had spent most of his life at a desk keeping records for a big company, had been tested both physically and mentally. On several occasions, wet, cold and tired, he had thought about quitting. But the persuasion of his guide, who had become a best friend, got him up the next mountain slope and kept him going.

Now, at long last, it was done. The stalk had been exhausting and exhilarating. The coolness he needed at the moment of truth, a coolness he had often wondered if he had, came through. Two well-placed shots put the magnificent animal down quickly and humanely.

His heart still raced as he sat on a cold, wet rock looking at the largest grizzly he had ever seen. Watching us clean up the trophy for pictures, Dawson tried to recapture the scene in his mind so he could remember it forever. He was filled with pride in his accomplishment, and he couldn't help but smile as he thought back to when, as a little freckled-faced boy, he used to read outdoor magazines and wish with all his might that he could someday visit some faraway wilderness and hunt a big bear.

Thanks to years of saving, months of planning and preparation, and a guide who wanted Dawson's dream to come true, it was now a reality. "Let's take some pictures," I called out.

Pulling his camera from his day pack, Dawson muttered, "Thank you, God, for big bear."

The History Of The Big Bear

According to scientists, giant bear existed in North America over one million years ago, but only their fossil remains could be found when bear as we know them first arrived. The brown-grizzly bear probably came from China during the Ice Age over the Bering Strait land bridge. The polar bear came along later and evolved from the brown bear of northern Russia.

North America's big bear are two of eight species of bear which are found in 90 countries around the world. The other bear are the black bear of North America, speckled bear of South America, Asiatic black bear found in Asia, sloth bear of India and surrounding countries and the sun bear found in east Asia.

Taxonomically, bear are members of the order *Carnivora*, or flesh-eating animals which range in size from the tiny least weasel up to the giant polar bear. A distinctive characteristic of this group of animals is their four long canine teeth that are used for seizing prey and stabbing their victims.

There had been a great deal of confusion in North America over what to call the brown-grizzly bear and how many different species exist. This confusion was not only among hunters, but wildlife biologists and scientists as well. The scientific community has finally concluded that the brown bear and the grizzly bear are the same species with the scientific name *Ursus arctos*.

The difference in size of bear within this species is due to diet. Because of their high protein diet of salmon, the large coastal bear, commonly called brown bear, may grow to be 1,500 pounds or more; their inland brothers, commonly called grizzlies, generally weigh only up to 800 pounds.

There are only two sub-species of *Ursus arctos*. The brown-grizzly bear found on Kodiak, Afognak and Shuyak Islands are *Ursus arctos middendorffi*. All other brown-grizzly bear are

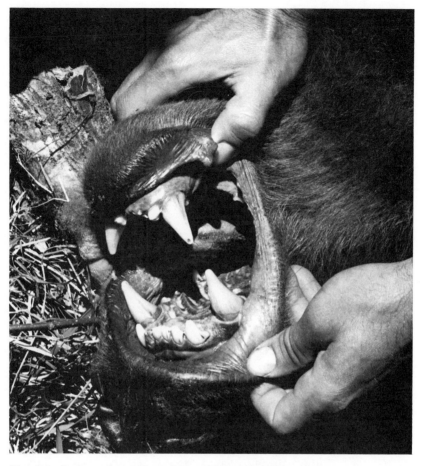

Bear have large canine teeth used for seizing and stabbing their prey.

Ursus arctos horribilis. Because of the difference in sizes of brown-grizzly bear found along the Alaskan coast, some hunter awards programs break the brown-grizzly bear into two categories: brown bear and grizzly bear. We'll cover that in detail in Chapter 12 on trophies.

Because these names are the commonly-accepted terminology used by most hunters and guides, I use "brown bear" and "grizzly bear" in this book to discuss the large coastal bear and smaller inland bear, respectively. This also keeps with the Boone & Crockett scoring system. But, please be aware that they are scientifically the same species.

The term "grizzly" probably comes from the mature bear's silver-tipped hair, or "grizzled" appearance. Early writers referred to the bear as a "grisly." Early explorers most often referred to the grizzly as the "white bear," and later many hunters, including Theodore Roosevelt, called it "Old Ephraim" or "ol' Eph," a commonly-used name for the devil. However, some mountain men called it "grizzly," as is seen in Osborne Russell's book *Journal of a Trapper*. Mexicans called it "oso grande!"

Nomenclature of the polar bear is far less confusing. Its scientific name is *Ursus maritimus*. Its first common name, Nanook, is what it is still called by Eskimos. It was English explorers who gave it the name "polar bear."

Distribution Of Big Bear

The distribution of the polar bear has changed very little over time. Their range covers the top of the world. In North America, polar bear are found along the Arctic coastal regions from the Seward Peninsula of Alaska east to Labrador and south along the shores of Hudson Bay to James Bay.

Distribution of the grizzly has changed greatly since the first Europeans came to North America. At that time, the range of the grizzly was extensive, covering Alaska, the Yukon, much of the Northwest Territories, British Columbia, Alberta, Saskatchewan and most of Manitoba. In the lower 48 states, its range included all the western states east to the western edge of Minnesota and Iowa, most of Kansas and the western half of Oklahoma and Texas. In Mexico, grizzly bear were found in the northern part of Baja, California and down through the central backbone of the country to Durango.

As civilization closed in on the grizzly range, the bear were usually the first to go, due in part to an exaggerated reputation for being dangerous and in part to the grizzlies taking an occasional head of livestock for a meal. In many areas, they were forced to retreat simply because towns, ranches, railroads and highways invaded their solitude.

Contrary to what many anti-hunters say, the demise of the grizzly in the lower 48 was not the doing of sport hunters. The grizzly was shot, trapped and poisoned at every opportunity by those with business interests rather than by sport hunters. In fact, it has only been in fairly recent times that the grizzly has received recognition as a game animal to be managed.

The difference in size of the coastal brown bear and the inland grizzly is attributed to the coastal bear's high-protein diet of salmon.

Today, the range of grizzly bear is far less than what it was originally. There are few, if any, grizzlies left in Mexico. In the lower 48 states, the grizzlies survive in six small areas:

1) In and adjacent to Yellowstone National Park.
2) Glacier National Park and the wilderness areas and associated lands south to the Blackfoot drainage and northwest to the Kootenai drainage in Montana.
3) The Cabinet Mountains and Yaak River drainage in the northwest corner of Montana.
4) The Bitterroot Mountains and associated wilderness lands north of the Salmon River and west to the Selway drainage in northern Idaho.
5) The Selkirk Mountains in northeast Washington and the panhandle of Idaho.
6) The northern edge of the Cascade Mountains in western Washington.

Considering the Lower 48, only in Montana is there a hunting season for grizzlies. It is a very limited season which is based on a quota system.

The grizzly range in Canada has been reduced to western Alberta, British Columbia, the Yukon and northern and western parts of the Northwest Territories. Grizzly hunting is very limited and restricted in Alberta and the Northwest Territories. It is still permitted in the Yukon and British Columbia by residents and non-residents.

The bright spot for grizzlies in North America is Alaska, where the range is still about the same as when the first Europeans arrived, with the exception of areas inhabited by man. The bear's population is still high, and hunting by both residents and non-residents is permitted.

The Grizzly And The American Indian

A vast majority of American Indians avoided contact with big bear because they believed that bear had supernatural powers. For example, some tribes thought that the bear caused evil. They killed bear only in self-defense, and no bear meat was eaten nor were the bear skinned. These tribes believed that they would get sick if they came in contact with the track of a bear, a tree where a bear had leaned or bear manure. Likewise, they believed that if they slept where a bear had sat down or came in contact with a bear by smell or touch, they would get sick.

Indians of the Pacific Northwest firmly believed in the supernatural powers of the grizzly, and the image of the bear was included in many totem poles. One of the most important clans among the Haida Indians was the Bear clan. According to legend, the clan originated when a woman was captured and taken as a wife by the king of bear, by whom she had a half-human and half-bear child. She was finally rescued by a group of hunters. Thus, the descendants of the child were members of the Bear clan.

Many other tribes also had bear cults. One human bear cult was in the Assiniboin Indians of Montana. It was composed of a small number of men who had obtained supernatural bear powers through dreams. This bear power could not be transferred to fellow tribesmen nor inherited by descendants after death. When a cult member died, his power went with him.

The Assiniboin Indians feared grizzlies, as they had lost a number of women and children to bear when they were out picking berries. Because of this fear of grizzlies, they also feared members of the bear cult.

Members of the bear cult wore a distinctive shirt, hair dress and face paint and carried a bear shield and bear knife with a handle fashioned from a bear paw. They lived in tepees on which they painted bear, conducted ceremonies in honor of the grizzly and sang bear songs. Since bear loved berries, they were the favorite food of the members of the Bear clan. The members observed a strict taboo against eating bear meat.

A major part of the ceremony to honor the grizzly was a symbolic bear hunt. A Bear clan member would erect his tepee, symbolic of a bear den, inside the camp circle of tepees. Dressed like a bear, he would emerge from his den carrying a bear knife in each hand. Other members on horseback would ride in and pretend to shoot the bear. The man dressed as a bear would fall down as though wounded, then get up and chase the mounted hunters until he made a complete circle of the camp, then return to his tepee.

When a member of the bear cult went to war against an enemy, he wore his distinctive bear outfit. Since bear were known for their ferocious charges, so was the Bear clan, complete with making noises like a grizzly. Some Indian tribes believed that bear were deceased family members or spirits of other important tribe members. Other tribes believed that if warriors ate vital parts of a grizzly, they would have the courage of the bear.

There is little doubt as to the importance of the grizzly in the lives of the western Indians, as many of the great warriors took the

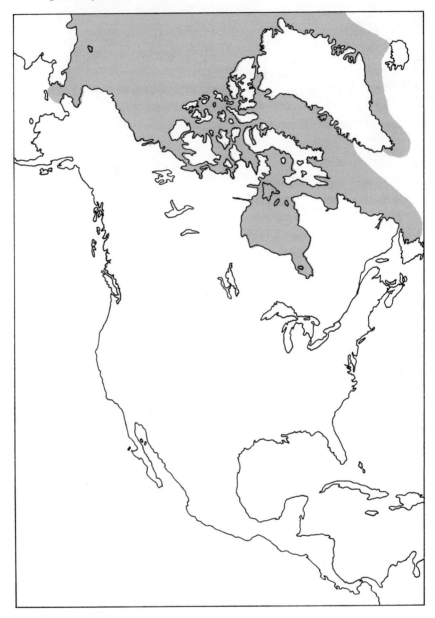

Polar bear range includes the Arctic coastal regions from the Seward Peninsula of Alaska east to Labrador and south along the shores of Hudson Bay to James Bay.

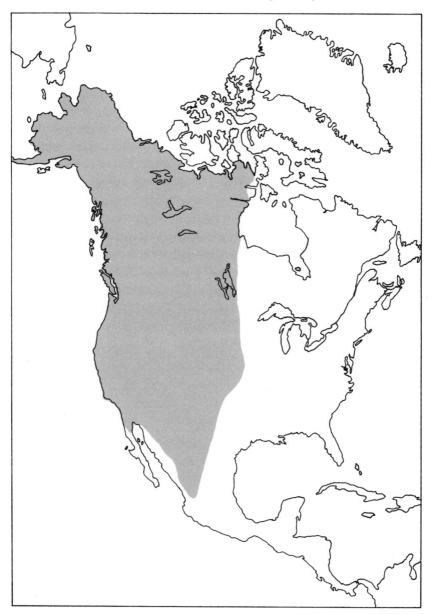

Pristine grizzly bear range.

Current grizzly bear range.

bear as their namesake. Bear, Bear Tooth, Bear Wolf, Strong Bear, Sleeping Bear, Bear's Backbone and Big Bear are some typical Indian names.

Many parts of the bear were used in Indian religious rites and by medicine men, but no part of the bear had more meaning than the claws. A necklace made from grizzly claws was the most treasured symbol of courage and bravery, and it was the most prized possession of the warrior who wore it. Even today it gets a lot of attention. I had a necklace made for my wife from the claws of a grizzly I shot. It gets the most attention of any jewelry she wears.

While most Indians had a live-and-let-live attitude toward grizzlies, some did hunt the bear for meat, skin and parts necessary for healing and ceremonies. When the hunt did occur it was always a group hunt, for with primitive weapons they knew that one lone Indian was no match against a grizzly. The hunt group was usually a half dozen or so warriors. As guns arrived in the West, Indians began to hunt bear in smaller numbers. Even then, the bear was a formidable foe.

J.W. Schultz, who lived with the Blackfeet, tells in his book, *My Life as an Indian,* of one grizzly hunt he made with his friend Heavy Breast. As he tells the story, they had just spotted a large grizzly tearing up a hillside in search of a gopher:

"We rode along in the edge of the timber down under the hill, my companion praying, promising the Sun an offering, and begging for success. At the foot of the hill we turned into a deep coulee and followed it up until we thought we were near the place where we had seen the bear; then we rode up out of it, and there was the old fellow not 50 yards away. He saw us as quickly as we did him, sat up on his haunches and wiggled his nose as he sniffed the air. We both fired and with a hair-lifting roar the bear rolled over, biting and clawing at his flank where a bullet had struck him, and then springing to his feet he charged us open-mouthed. We both urged our horses off to the north, for it was not wise to turn back down the hill. I fired a couple of shots as fast as I could, but without effect. The bear meantime had covered the ground with surprisingly long bounds, and was already close to the heels of my companion's horse. I fired again and made another miss, and just then Heavy Breast, his saddle and his sheep meat parted company with the fleeing pony; the cinch, an old, worn, rawhide band, had broken.

" 'Hi ya', my friend!' he cried, pleadingly, as he soared up in the air, still astride the saddle. Down they came with a loud thud not two steps in front of the onrushing bear, and that animal, with a dismayed and frightened 'woof,' turned sharply about and fled back toward the timber, with me after him. I kept firing, and finally a lucky shot broke his backbone; it was easy then to finish him with a deliberately aimed bullet in the base of the brain. When it was all over I suddenly remembered how ridiculous Heavy Breast had appeared soaring on a horseless saddle, and how his eyes bulged as he called upon me for aid. I began to laugh and it seemed as if I never could stop. My companion had come up beside me and stood, very solemn, looking at me and the bear."

Occasionally an Indian would prove his bravery by going after a grizzly alone. One such hunt was recorded by the missionary Ignaz Pfefferkorn in 1795 when he wrote *The Grizzly in the Southwest.*

"The Sonora bear looks just as bold and frightful as the European bear, which it resembles in body shape, size, strength, and savagery. However, it does no harm to man because it finds enough to eat in the woods and meadows. If a man attacks it, however, its rage is frightful. I was once a sorrowful witness to this. A brave Indian took me on a journey, and on the way we saw pass us a terrible bear, on its way to hide itself in the nearby mountains. While I continued with my company, the bold Indian remained behind and, unbeknownst to me, followed the ferocious animal. He caught up with the bear as it was climbing the mountain and wounded it badly, as we afterwards saw from its bloody tracks. But thereupon the infuriated animal attacked him and tore him to pieces. These we found lying about him when we turned back to look for him."

All things considered, the Indian and the grizzly had mutual respect for one another and generally got along well while sharing the same area.

Explorers And Big Bear

While explorers and missionaries in the Southwest and fur traders in the Far North had already encountered grizzlies, it was the Lewis and Clark Expedition that first brought the grizzly to the attention of the colonies in the early 1800s. Members of the expedition had numerous encounters with the "white bear." A retreat up a tree or into a river was often the only course of action. Due to these early encounters and warnings from the Indians about

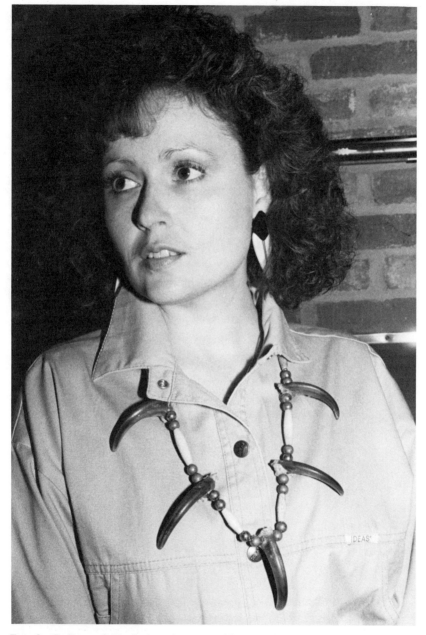

For the Indians of North America, a necklace made from grizzly claws was a treasured symbol of courage and bravery. Today, grizzly claws still make an impressive necklace.

For North America's early mountain men, the grizzly was a formidable opponent. While these fur trappers were known for spinning tall tales, there is little doubt that the essence of their grizzly reports is true.

the threat from the big bear, expedition reports tended to overemphasize the danger posed by the grizzly.

The next series of reports on the ferocity of the big bear came from the fur trappers who came to be called "mountain men." While mountain men were known for spinning tall tales, there is little doubt that at least the essence of their grizzly reports is true.

Manuel Lisa and other trappers wintering at Fort Raymond in 1807 felt the wrath of the big bear when grizzlies got into their meat storage and ate all the meat on hand. Had nearby game not been plentiful, this would have been a serious loss. Nonetheless, this gave the grizzly the reputation of being a thief to be shot on sight.

George Frederick Ruxton was a trapper who wrote about the trapper's life. Here is how he reported on the grizzly in *Ruxton of the Rockies*:

"The grizzly bear is the fiercest of the *ferae naturae* of the mountains. His great strength and wonderful tenacity of life render an encounter with him anything but desirable, and therefore it is a rule with the Indians and white hunters never to attack him unless backed by a strong party. Although, like every other wild animal, he usually flees from man, yet at certain seasons, when maddened by love or hunger, he not infrequently charges at first sight of a foe, when, unless killed dead, a hug at close quarters is anything but a pleasant embrace, his strong hooked claws stripping the flesh from bones as easily as a cook peels an onion. Many are the tales of bloody encounters with these animals which the trappers delight to recount to the greenhorn, to enforce their caution as to the foolhardiness of ever attacking the grizzly bear.''

No other hunting story told during the early 1800s did more to turn man against grizzlies than did the many versions of the Hugh Glass mauling. No one ever found out the truth of the story, but Ruxton's version is the one most repeated even today. Here is how Ruxton wrote about it in *Ruxton of the Rockies*:

"Some years ago a trapping party was on their way to the mountains, led, I believe, by old Sublette, a well-known captain of the West. Amongst the band was one John (Hugh) Glass, a trapper who had been all his life in the mountains, and had seen, probably, more exciting adventures, and had had more wonderful and hairbreadth escapes, than any of the rough and hardy fellows who make the West their home, and whose lives are spent in a succession of perils and privations. On one of the streams running from the Black Hills, a range of mountains northward of the Platte, Glass and a companion were one day setting their traps, when, on passing through a cherry thicket which skirted the stream, the former, who was in advance, described a large grizzly bear quietly turning up the turf with his nose, searching for yampa roots or pig nuts, which there abounded. Glass immediately called his companion, and both, proceeding cautiously, crept to the skirt of the thicket, and, taking steady aim at the animal, whose broadside was fairly exposed at the distance of twenty yards, discharged their rifles at the same instant, both balls taking effect, but not inflicting a mortal wound. The bear, giving a groan of pain, jumped with all four legs from the ground, and, seeing the wreaths of smoke hanging at the edge of the brush, charged at once in that direction, snorting with pain and fury.

" 'Harraw, Bill!' roared out Glass, as he saw the animal rushing towards them, 'we'll be made meat of as sure as shootin'!' and, leaving the tree behind which he had concealed himself, he bolted through the thicket, followed closely by his companion. The brush was so thick that they could scarcely make their way through, whereas the weight and strength of the bear carried him through all obstructions, and he was soon close upon them.

"About 100 yards from the thicket was a steep bluff, and between these points was a level piece of prairie; Glass saw that his only chance was to reach this bluff, and, shouting to his companion to make for it, they both broke from the cover and flew like lightning across the open space. When more than half way across, the bear being about 50 yards behind them, Glass, who was leading, tripped over a stone and fell to the ground, and just as he rose to his feet, the beast, rising on his hind feet, confronted him. As he closed, Glass, never losing his presence of mind, cried to his companion to load up quickly, and discharged his pistol full into the body of the animal, at the same moment that the bear, with blood streaming from its nose and mouth, knocked the pistol from his hand with one blow of its paw, and, fixing its claws deep into his flesh, rolled with him to the ground.

"The hunter, notwithstanding his hopeless situation, struggled manfully, drawing his knife and plunging it several times into the body of the beast, which, furious with pain, tore with tooth and claw the body of the wretched victim, actually baring the ribs of flesh and exposing the very bones.

"Weak with loss of blood, and with eyes blinded with the blood which streamed from his lacerated scalp, the knife at length fell from his hand, and Glass sank insensible, and to all appearance dead.

"His companion, who, up to this moment, had watched the conflict, which, however, lasted but a few seconds, thinking that his turn would come next, and not having had presence of mind even to load his rifle, fled with might and main back to camp, where he narrated the miserable fate of poor Glass. The captain of the band of trappers, however, dispatched the man with a companion back to the spot where he lay, with instructions to remain by him if still alive, or to bury him if, as all supposed he was, defunct, promising them at the same time a sum of money for so doing.

"On reaching the spot, which was red with blood, they found Glass still breathing, and the bear, dead and stiff, actually lying upon his body. Poor Glass presented a horrifying spectacle: the flesh was torn in strips from his chest and limbs, and large flaps strewed the ground; his scalp hung bleeding over his face, which was also lacerated in a shocking manner.

"The bear, besides the three bullets which had pierced its body, bore the marks of the fierce nature of Glass's final struggle, no less than twenty gaping wounds in the breast and belly testifying to the gallant defense of the mountaineer.

"Imagining that, if not already dead, the poor fellow could not possibly survive more than a few moments, the men collected his arms, stripped him even of his hunting shirt and moccasins, and, merely pulling the dead bear off the body, mounted their horses, and slowly followed the remainder of the party, saying, when they reached it, that Glass was dead, as probably they thought, and that they had buried him.

"In a few days the gloom which pervaded the trappers' camp, occasioned by the loss of a favorite companion, disappeared, and Glass's misfortune, although frequently mentioned over the campfire, at length was almost entirely forgotten in the excitement of the hunt and Indian perils which surrounded them.

"Months elapsed, the hunt was over, and the party of trappers were on their way to the trading fort with their packs of beaver. It was nearly sundown, and the round adobe bastions of the mud-built fort were just in sight, when a horseman was seen slowly approaching them along the banks of the river. When near enough to discern his figure they saw a lank cadaverous form with a face so scarred and disfigured that scarcely a feature was discernible. Approaching the leading horsemen, one whom happened to be the companion of the defunct Glass in his memorable bear scrape, the stranger, in a hollow voice, reining in his horse before them, exclaimed, 'Harraw, Bill, my boy! You thought I was gone under that time, did you? But hand me over my horse and gun, my lad; I ain't dead yet by a dam sight!' "

With the spreading of this story, the grizzly bear was considered one of the western explorers' greatest menaces, second only to Indians. According to historian Robert G. Cleland, few trapping expeditions returned from the mountains without having lost some of their members to grizzly attacks.

Another mountain man, Osborne Russell, wrote a journal of his adventures in which he tells of the problems with the grizzly, the first being in 1834, his first year as a trapper. The book, *Journal of a Trapper (1834-1843) Osborne Russell* was edited by Aubrey L. Haines.

"On the 20th of August we started again to hunt meat: we left the Fort and travelled about six miles when we discovered a Grizzly Bear digging and eating roots in a piece of marshy ground near a large bunch of willows. The Mullattoe approached within 100 yards and shot him through the left shoulder. He gave a hideous growl and sprang into the thicket. The Mullattoe then said, 'Let him go. He is a dangerous varmint,' but not being acquainted with the nature of these animals I determined on making another trial, and persuaded the Mullattoe to assist me we walked round the bunch of willows where the bear lay keeping close together, with our rifles ready cocked and presented towards the bushes until near the place where he had entered, when we heard a sullen growl about 10 feet from us, which was instantly followed by a spring of the bear toward us; his enormous jaws extended and eyes flashing fire.

"Oh Heavens! Was ever anything so hideous? We could not retain sufficient presence of mind to shoot at him but took to our heels separating as we ran the bear taking after me, finding I could out run him he left and turned to the other who wheeled about and discharged his rifle covering the bear with smoke and fire the ball however further without jumping into a large quagmire which hemmed me on three sides, I was obliged to turn about and face him he came within about 10 paces of me then suddenly stopped and raised his ponderous body erect, his mouth wide open, gazing at me with a beastly laugh at this moment I pulled trigger and I knew not what else to do and hardly knew that I did this but it accidentally happened that my rifle was pointed towards the bear when I pulled and the ball piercing his heart, he gave one bound from me uttered a deathly howl and fell dead: but I trembled as if I had an ague fit for half an hour after, we butchered him as he was very fat packed the meat and skin on our horses and returned to the Fort with the trophies of our bravery, but I secretly determined in my own mind never to molest another wounded Grizzly Bear in a marsh or thicket."

On another occasion Russell recorded this account:

"We stopped to approach a band of buffalo and as myself and one of my comrades (a Canadian) were walking along half bent near some bushes secreting ourselves from the buffalo a large Grizzly Bear who probably had been awakened from his slumbers by our approach sprang upon the Canadian who was five or six feet before me and placing one forepaw upon his head and the other on his left shoulder pushed him one side about 12 feet with as little ceremony as if he had been a cat still keeping a direct course as tho nothing had happened. I called to the Canadian and soon found the fright exceeded the wound as he had received no injury except

During the 1800s, grizzly bear were found in large numbers throughout most of the Northwest.

what this impudent stranger had done by tearing his coat but it was hard telling which was the most frightened the man or the Bear.''

Russell reported that the flesh of the grizzly bear was preferable to pork. His comments in *Journal of a Trapper (1834-1843) Osborne Russell* concerning the grizzly bear ended by saying, ''It will generally run from the scent of man but when it does not get the scent it will often let him approach close enough to spring upon him and when wounded it is a dangerous animal to trifle with.''

Apparently not everyone thought the grizzly bear to be a bad critter, as the crew of the steamboat Assiniboin kept a pair of grizzly cubs on board for a period of time.

The grizzly bear was numerous in most of the western states throughout much of the 1800s. In Robert Glass Cleland's *This Reckless Breed of Men: The Trappers and Fur Traders of The Southwest*, mountain man George G. Yount made this claim: ''They were everywhere—upon the plains, in the valleys and on the mountains, so that I have often killed as many as five or six in one day and it is not unusual to see 50 or 60 within the 24 hours.''

Explorer and writer George Bird Grinnell wrote of multiple sightings in 1874. His work appears in *The Passing of the Great West: Selected Papers of George Bird Grinnell,* which was edited by John F. Reiger.

"One day just before leaving the Hills, Captain North, when three or four miles off to one side of the command, saw no less than five bear traveling along together on the prairie half a mile distant. If he had had a horse that could run, he might have attempted to kill some of them. About this time the Sioux, Cold Hand, and a young Ree came on an old grizzly bear and two yearling cubs, which they attacked. The bear ran out toward the prairie, and the Indians followed on horseback. They killed first one cub and then the other, but the mother kept far ahead of them. Finally their horses gave out and could carry them no further. Cold Hand, a cripple, could not go on, but the young Ree kept after the old bear on foot and finally killed her in a water hole where she had taken refuge.''

James H. "Captain Jim" Cook, famous hunter and scout, was also a writer and recorded this interesting story. It appears in his book, *Fifty Years on the Old Frontier.*

"Late in the fall of 1880, I guided a party of Englishmen on a hunting trip into the Big Horn Mountains of Wyoming. We found plenty of game—elk, buffalo, deer, and mountain sheep being there in abundance. Bear also were unusually plentiful, and we had some great sport hunting them.

"One morning I started out with two of the party on a bear hunt. It was their first hunt, and they had never seen a bear in its wild state. As still-hunting bear usually requires the utmost skill, I had little hope of success; especially as the heavy hob-nailed shoes worn by the Englishmen made so much noise against the rocks that I was sure we should not be able to get within gunshot of a bear. When we reached the place where I knew there was good bear ground, I instructed the men to move, in line with me, very slowly and carefully through the thick timber, to keep within sight of me, and also, if they saw any animal, to beckon me to them.

"When we had moved along cautiously in this manner for perhaps a quarter of a mile, one of the Englishmen motioned to me to come to him. When I reached his side he said that he had seen what he thought was a hog enter a little thicket about 100 yards distant. Knowing that there was not a hog within a hundred miles of us, I was sure he had seen a bear. Looking the ground over carefully, I could see where we could get to a low, rocky point of land that overlooked the thicket into which the strange animal had gone. Backing slowly away until out of sight, we slipped around to the point. Reaching there, I peered over into the thicket. In a few minutes I saw a bear within 50 yards of me. He was digging into the ground after some food, and, as I observed that he was not alarmed, I watched him several minutes.

"Suddenly I thought I saw something move in a clump of brush a short distance from the bear. Changing my position a few inches, and watching the place, I caught sight of a very large silvertip grizzly lying down. Just as I made this discovery, to my astonishment three more bear put in an appearance. They slouched up to the bear which was digging into the ground, and he snarled at the newcomers as if warning them not to disturb him in his efforts to secure food. I motioned for my companions to slip up beside me, and they soon had a view of the bear.

"The Englishmen were armed with double-barreled express rifles of heavy bore. I whispered to them that I would shoot the big bear which was lying down, and that, the moment I fired, they were to open up on any of the others that were in good positions for shooting. I shot the big fellow, and at the report of my rifle he tried to rise, screaming with pain and rage. The one of the bear which was nearest my victim immediately sprang upon the wounded animal and began to bite him. The Englishmen began shooting at once, but the bear, instead of trying to escape, sprang at each other like demons, fighting and growling savagely. In less than a minute those four bear were merged into one struggling heap, into which we poured shot after shot. The big fellow which I had shot first was out of the battle entirely.

"Presently the smallest animal broke away from the others and ran about 50 yards, as fast as he could streak it. Climbing up on a fallen log, he rose on his hind legs and stood looking back at the battle, which was still raging with unabated fury. He offered a beautiful mark; I shot him through the heart, and he dropped off the log with a yell.

"One after another, the remaining bear went down under our rain of bullets, each hit not less than 10 or 12 times. It was an exciting scene. My English friends were greatly elated, and I myself had witnessed a sight such as I never would have dreamed could be. Very seldom are five bear found together by a hunter, and their reason for flying at each other in such a savage manner, paying no attention whatever either to the reports of our rifles or to ourselves, was inexplicable.

"When we packed the hides of those five silvertip grizzlies back to camp that evening, we certainly had something to talk about."

The large numbers of grizzlies were not to last long. As civilization moved west, cattle, sheep and other livestock made easy meals for the bear. Grizzlies clashed with mining camps, logging camps, railroad camps and small towns that were springing up everywhere. Due to the tremendous amount of publicity given the bear about their "man-killing" ways, every bear was killed on sight. By the early 1900s, professional hunters were brought into many areas to exterminate the beast. The bear was chased by hounds, trapped and poisoned. There was no limit to how much effort the bear killers would expend to carry out their mission.

In 1911, Ben Lilly, a much publicized hunter, and his Airedale dog jumped a large grizzly just out of hibernation in New Mexico. He trailed the bear, which had two toes missing, into the San Louis Mountains in the state of Chihuahua, Mexico.

Lilly returned to the United States side of the border to pick up supplies, and two weeks later, went back to the mountains to pick up the trail. Soon after picking up the trail, Lilly caught the bear for a few moments in a trap, but the animal dragged the trap and got away. He then trailed the bear into the state of Sonora, Mexico, before it returned to the San Louis Mountains. Soon thereafter, as the bear was making its way to the Animas Mountains, Lilly killed it. He had followed the bear through three states in two countries.

Not all bear hunters were so lucky. James "Bear" Moore, a professional hunter in New Mexico, shot a large grizzly in the back while hunting alone one morning. The bear dropped as though dead. When Moore went to check his kill, the bear was waiting. A fellow hunter found Moore that night with his face ripped away and his jaw torn loose. His chest had been ripped open and his heart was exposed. Somehow he was still alive. The grizzly lay dead nearby with its stomach ripped open. Moore's knife lay on the ground next to him. Miraculously, Moore survived but was so disfigured that he became a recluse.

The grizzly gradually began disappearing from the western United States. Within a period of 100 years, the grizzly population diminished to only a fraction of its earlier number, victims of so-called "progress." No thought had been given to the

The polar bear's triangular body shape is ideal for cutting through water. It can swim up to 60 miles without resting, averaging six miles per hour.

management of these magnificent creatures as a resource. This would be left for the next generation.

Fortunately, the upcoming generation saw the big bear as a valuable game animal that should be managed as such, and wildlife managers began to study these interesting animals.

Physiology

For many years, the big brown bear found on Kodiak Island were thought to be the largest of bear, with recorded weights of up to 1,656 pounds and heights as tall as 11 feet.

But it is now thought that polar bear may be larger, as a rule, as one is on record at over 11 feet tall and 2,210 pounds. Of course, this is an exceptional bear, and most polar bear taken by hunters fall in the eight- to 10-foot range. Mature males generally weigh between 600 and 1,200 pounds, and females 400 to 700 pounds. They stand about four feet high at the shoulder.

The polar bear color is not pure white, as many people think, but is actually a yellowish-cream color. Each hair is hollow, insulating the bear from the extreme cold of its habitat. Its black nose stands out against the near-white background, and bear stalking seals have been observed placing a paw over the nose to camouflage it.

The polar bear's body shape is that of a sharp triangle with the apex at the nose, an ideal shape for cutting through water. The tapering head acts like the bow of a ship. When swimming, only the front feet, which are webbed, are used for paddling. The rear feet are used like rudders for steering. The polar bear can swim up to 60 miles without resting at an average speed of six miles per hour.

The polar bear must propel himself onto floating ice to capture unsuspecting seals. These leaps can be as much as eight feet into the air from a swimming start.

The eyesight of the polar bear is much better than that of other bear, and they have stiff hair on the bottoms of their feet to keep them from slipping on the ice.

While the largest coastal brown bear are 10 feet or more in length and weigh well over 1,000 pounds, the average is in the 800- to 1,000-pound range. Those measuring over 10 feet in length are getting harder to come by, and most hunters are glad to get a nine-foot bear. A large brown bear stands about 4½ feet high at the shoulder.

Exceptional inland grizzlies may weigh up to 900 pounds, but the average is in the range of 400 to 800 pounds with an average length of six to eight feet. They average 3½ feet high at the shoulder. Females weigh one-half to three-quarters as much.

The brown-grizzly bear resembles its close relative, the black bear. The brown-grizzly is usually larger, with a prominent shoulder hump and longer, straighter claws. In profile, the brown-grizzly face is concave between the forehead and the nose.

Color is not a very reliable way to differentiate between these bear, for both species have many color phases. Brown-grizzly bear colors range from dark brown through blonde. Black bear colors range from black through many hues of brown to blonde.

All of the big bear have 42 teeth: 12 incisors, four canines, 16 premolars and 10 molars. Bear are the only large predators that regularly eat both plants and meat; therefore, they have both meat-eating and plant-eating teeth in their mouths. The molars are for grinding plant food, and the canine and incisor teeth are for catching and killing animals. The canine teeth of the polar bear are longer than those of the other big bear.

Bear are related to dogs, foxes and wolves with a similar skeleton, except that the bones are larger and much heavier. Laced to this skeleton are massive muscles. The bear has a strong, unusually large heart, and they have been known to survive injuries that would kill any other animal.

Inland grizzlies like this one stand six to eight feet tall and weigh from 400 to 800 pounds. Large coastal brown bear, meanwhile, may stand 10 feet tall and weigh well over 1,000 pounds.

Contrary to popular opinion, big bear like water and are good swimmers.

The long claws on the front feet, some up to five inches, make the bear a formidable enemy and are very effective at digging up food or catching fish.

The body of the big bear may look fat and clumsy, but these animals are among the strongest and fastest on earth, running at speeds up to 40 miles an hour. They can cover a distance of 150 yards in 10 seconds—a fact all hunters should keep in mind. They also have tremendous endurance. I once interviewed an old grizzly hunter who had used dogs to hunt down grizzlies earlier in this century. He said that on several occasions he had chased a grizzly for 30 miles before it came to bay.

A common myth about the big bear is that they can't run downhill. Wrong! They can run downhill or uphill easily and quickly.

Due to the weight of a mature brown-grizzly bear and the length of its claws, they have a hard time climbing trees, often preferring to shake its intended victim down or wait it out before attempting to climb. But as many hunters have learned the hard way, if the tree has limbs close enough for the bear to grab them, he will come on up.

There are also those who think a heavy bear can't swim. Don't you believe it; they are excellent swimmers and can tolerate water much colder than a man can survive in.

Another misconception is that bear have very poor eyesight. I have heard people say with authority that bear are nearly blind. The bear biologists I have talked to disagree. In fact, most think the bear's eyesight is as good as man's. They can see colors, form and movement, but apparently prefer to rely on their more acute senses of smell and hearing.

The temperament of the big bear is one of their least understood characteristics. Basically, they are wilderness loners and don't want anything to do with man or other bear, except for mating or rearing cubs. Each bear, much more so than other members of the wild kingdom, seems to have its own personality. What one bear will do, another won't. What a bear will do today, he won't do tomorrow. This is the reason you can never predict the behavior of a bear. They are known to possess a great amount of pride and dignity, and this alone has been suspected of causing some unsuspecting persons a lot of trouble. For example, a bear that is recovering from a fight with a larger bear may take his problems out on an unsuspecting person who happens along at the time.

Bear have been known to hold a grudge against people. A bear that has been wounded by one hunter may take it out on several other hunters. Recorded incidences demonstrate this.

While the polar bear may look at a man as just another large seal, the brown-grizzly is not generally a man-eater. When he attacks, which is not nearly as often as most believe, there is usually a good reason, such as being wounded, having cubs nearby, being startled, having food nearby, having his space invaded or just being mad at folks in general. If given a chance, most bear would rather just go their separate way.

The life span of big bear in the wild is from 20 to 25 years.

Food

The polar bear is the only one of the North American bear that is nearly a true carnivore. His diet consists mainly of ringed seals, which he catches by slipping up on them or leaping out of the water on them at the edges of ice.

They also wait for seals at breathing holes. Young seals, a special treat for the bear, are had by breaking into puppy chambers in snow on top of the ice in spring. Polar bear will also feed on bearded seals and carrion of whale, seal and walrus carcasses found along the coast. They occasionally eat small mammals, bird eggs and some vegetation when other food is not available.

It might be easier to name what the brown-grizzly bear won't eat than what he will. He is omnivorous. He likes all berries, green grass, horsetail, willow sedge, cow parsnip, pine nuts, fish, rodents, insects and roots of many plants.

He likes domestic or game animals when he can get them, but he is probably not a significant predator on big game animals except during the spring moose and caribou calving season.

The brown-grizzly bear especially likes carrion and will feed on carcasses of animals. Occasionally, he turns to cannibalism, especially liking small cubs. However, some wildlife biologists report that 90 percent of the bear's diet is vegetable matter. In settled areas, they will even eat garbage. I have learned the hard way that they like bacon, left-over bannock, beans, steak and most other camp foods, including canned goods.

Biologists have found that brown-grizzly and polar bear may consume as much as 90 pounds of food per day.

Life Cycle

There are two times when mature male bear break with their solitary lifestyles. One is when food is abundant near other bear, and the other is when it's time to mate. Both polar and brown-grizzly bear breed in the spring. The polar bear's breeding season is March, April and May. Males actively seek out females by following their tracks on the sea ice. Brown-grizzly mating takes place from May through July, with the peak of activity in June. Big bear do not have strong ties, and a male will not stay with a female for long.

All female bear that breed have what biologists call "delayed implantation." That is, even though they breed in late spring or early summer, the fertilized egg does not implant in the uterus until October or November. Biologists believe this to be a survival mechanism in that the embryo will not develop unless the sow is healthy and has sufficient fat reserved to last the winter and to care for the cubs. Delayed implantation and the short, six- to eight-week embryo development period means that the cubs are surprisingly small at birth, usually around one pound each.

The long claws on a grizzly's front feet are very effective when gathering or catching food, and when used in a battle.

Once the mating is completed, bear go their separate ways. As winter approaches, the bear begin to locate suitable denning sites. Polar bear seek out dens in late October and November, with most denning on land, but some on heavy sea ice. They seek the lee side of icebergs, steep hillside slopes where snow drifts persist, or the lee side of lake or stream banks where deep snow drifts accumulate.

Brown-grizzly bear usually locate their denning sites by late October, often selecting a site where the entrance is below a stand of willows or alders so that the hanging branches will cover the opening and catch the snow. Dens are sometimes found on north-facing slopes where snow drifts are deeper.

Dens are usually located in soil that is soft enough for digging. The chamber is egg-shaped and large enough to allow the bear some room for stretching during the winter. It must be small enough, however, that the airspace will be efficiently warmed by the bear.

The winter dormancy period of bear differs from that of most other mammal hibernators because the body temperature does not drop. Brown-grizzly bear can remain inactive in dens for up to seven months by reducing their heart rate, metabolism functions, oxygen consumption and blood circulation. Among polar bear, pregnant females are the only ones that den for long periods of time.

Young bear are born from late November through February. Except for the polar bear, the cubs are born virtually naked. They require a great deal of care from their mother. The polar bear will most often have a litter of two, and the brown-grizzly litter may be from one to four, with an average of two.

Female polar bear and cubs break out of the den in late March or early April when the cubs weigh about 15 pounds. They make short trips to and from the den until the cubs become acclimated to the outside temperatures. Then they start traveling on the drifting sea ice. The cubs stay with their mother until they are about 28 months old. Females can breed again at about the time they separate from their cubs, so they generally produce litters every third year.

Brown-grizzly bear emerge from the den in about April, depending upon the weather. Females with cubs emerge later than single bear. The cubs remain with their mother through their second year, and then the female will breed again.

Polar bear breed from March through May. A male polar bear will locate a female by following the scent in her tracks on the sea ice.

Grizzly bear have a slow reproduction rate. It will take the female bear five to seven years to reach sexual maturity. The sow will be a constant teacher for her cubs during their first two years.

Newborn cubs are highly dependent on their mother for protection from all dangers, including large male bear, which occasionally kill and eat cubs. The mother teaches her cubs hunting and feeding techniques. They learn to recognize predators and to locate suitable denning sites. The mother is a very strict disciplinarian and quickly stops misbehavior with a hard blow from her paw.

During the second winter, the cubs den with their mother. They are then chased off in the spring, as the mother is ready to breed again.

The big bear usually become sexually mature at between five and seven years of age.

Daily movement of brown-grizzly bear is influenced by temperatures, as you would be if you had on a heavy, dark brown coat and were out in the sun for long periods. They move and feed during the cool evening and morning hours. They often prefer to feed in shady areas, making it harder for the hunter to spot them.

Habitat

The habitat of the polar bear is the Arctic ice pack and surrounding coastal areas. For the brown-grizzly bear, it is much more varied. When big bear descend from their dens in the spring in search of berries and grasses, they like river banks, flood plains and tidal flats. While a few bear use river shore trails and surrounding habitat during the early summer, they do not begin to concentrate there until berries, such as soapberries, ripen and later when the salmon runs begin. Forest areas are used by the big bear for shade and some food. But since many of the forests are so dense, the sunlight is restricted from reaching the forest floor, and adequate growth of vegetation suitable for food is limited.

In regions where a variety of forest and meadow types are found, there is a better supply of bear food than in the vast expanse of trees. Bear will feed in the meadows and make daybeds in the forest margins adjacent to open areas.

Where the forest thins at higher elevations and on snow slides, the slopes support shrubs, bushes and small, scattered tree growth. This is good grizzly habitat.

Emerging greens adjacent to melting snow and moist creek edges are especially good for bear feeding. Roots, berries and ground squirrels make up the remainder of their diet.

The vast, open tundra is also home to the brown-grizzly bear. This barren ground, which on first appearance seems void of any life, offers the big bear grasses, sedges, small mammals and, in some cases, caribou calves as food. Cover and shade are found in alder and willow thickets along creeks and lakes.

Management

Big bear management knowledge is many years behind that of other big game species in North America. The public attitude toward the big bear has been one of fear and dislike. This has changed, though somewhat slowly in some areas, and now wildlife officials are working to learn more about the management of bear. One factor that has to be taken into account, and one that many people don't consider, is their generally low rate of reproduction. We tend to think of all game animals like deer. A healthy doe will produce two fawns each year, beginning as a yearling. By contrast, there is usually a two- to three-year interval between litters in a female bear, and she takes five to seven years to reach sexual maturity. Also, bear reproduction can be greatly affected by food shortages. Females in poor condition do not reproduce.

Because of this slow reproductive rate, game and fish agencies must conduct extensive studies on the total bear population to recommend desirable types of hunting at intensities that will not over-harvest populations. Research studies each year include detailed assessments of harvest, movement patterns, population surveys and basic life-history studies.

It is studies of this type that have produced the quota system for the hunting of big bear. This system, which dictates the number of bear that can be harvested in a specific area, has helped in keeping the bear population at healthy numbers, yet allowing sportsmen to enjoy the resource.

Habitat conservation is another major part of any bear management program. Due to human development, the large tracts of wilderness required by big bear are ever-decreasing. Even where these vast areas exist, disturbances by man can have a major impact on bear. For example, an oil spill from a tanker in the Arctic may kill enough seals to lead to starvation of the polar bear in that area.

As more people invade bear habitat, the frequency of man-bear encounters is growing, and the bear is the ultimate loser. What most people in bear habitat don't realize is that they are in an area where man is not supreme. The need in any management plan is to guide human activities to avoid man-bear encounters. This may involve prohibiting man from using some areas at specific times.

As is pointed out in several places in this book, disturbance of bear habitat by roads, oil rigs, mining, low-level aircraft activity and other development forces bear into lower quality habitat where survival is difficult and reproduction is less successful. Land-controlling agencies must recognize that as a part of any big bear management program, restrictions on agriculture, logging, mining and oil development is required in bear habitat. Without this, especially in Alaska, huntable bear populations will decline.

Big bear management is a new science, and we still have much to learn about the management of these complex animals. We sportsmen can do our part by encouraging bear management programs and following hunting restrictions to the letter.

3

Planning
Your Bear Hunt

Bob Perry had spent 10 years saving for a once-in-a-lifetime grizzly hunt. Both he and his wife had worked hard to put aside enough money for his dream hunt. At last the account was sufficient to hire a guide, pay the airfare and cover the license cost.

Perry picked out three guides to call by looking at ads in several of his favorite outdoor magazines. He picked the guides by the size of their ads, allowing that the more successful the guide, the more he could spend for advertising. The first guide he called was polite but almost sounded as if he were talking him out of the hunt. He told Perry that his hunter success ran 60 percent on his last spring hunt. He pointed out that his hunts were hard, with days often spent in snowshoes.

He told Perry that his camps were comfortable but not a Hilton, and that there was an additional cost to fly from the nearest village served by commercial airlines to his base camp. Perry figured this must be a trapper picking up some side money by guiding in the spring.

The second guide he called sounded more like what he wanted. He told Perry that he achieved a 99 percent success rate every season on bear, and due to the abundance of bear in the area, he might have time to get in some fishing. The guide described the terrain as gentle and the camp as new and modern in every way. As the guide gave Perry three references, he assured him of success if he hunted with him.

Excited over what this guide had told him, Perry didn't bother to call the third one. Instead, he started calling the three references. The first reference was someone in Las Vegas. His report on the guide was that everything was excellent, first class, bear everywhere. His closing comment was that his brother-in-law ran the best hunting business in Alaska. The second reference was never home. The third reference was actually a fisherman who said that he had seen lots of bear sign when he fished with this guide.

In the meantime, the guide had sent Perry a brochure which showed pictures of bear and had many statements from hunters about how good the guide service was. Perry, running short of time, decided that the guide must be all right and sent him a 50 percent deposit.

That was the last Perry heard of his guide until about a month before the scheduled hunt when Perry called him to get information on clothing and hunting license. The guide told him to pack as if he were going on a whitetail deer hunt and he would be okay. He further told him that licenses were no problem and they would take care of those details when he got to Alaska.

Soon the time for the hunt arrived. Perry flew from his home in Kentucky to Anchorage, and from there to the small village near the guide's camp. The airport at the village was a small metal building, and when Perry arrived, there was no one to meet him. In fact, a few minutes after the commercial airliner departed, there was no one else at the building at all.

The locals who got off the plane had all gone, and Perry was left standing in the cold building, watching the snow fall outside and wondering what he should do.

Walking around, he came upon an aircraft mechanic working in a hanger adjacent to the small terminal. The mechanic knew where the guide's base camp was. He told Perry he was the local air taxi, but he couldn't take him out to the camp until the next morning. He suggested that Perry get a cab and go into the village to stay at Porter's Motel. Perry, somewhat bewildered at this point, had the mechanic call a cab, which turned out to be a beat-up pickup that cost $50 for the three-mile trip to the mobile home called Porter's Motel. The cold, somewhat less than clean, room cost $95 per night. The only cafe open charged eight bucks for a small hamburger.

Perry had not expected any of these costs, and they were eating

Bear hunts can't be thrown together within a month or two. Bear guides with good reputations are booked up to a year in advance. Cy Ford (right) is a British Columbia guide with a good reputation. In 1987, he was booked two years in advance. Picture shows Cy with Steve Garland and his giant grizzly which placed third in the Safari Club International record book.

into his extra cash. The next morning, after waiting around for two hours, he was wedged with his gear into the rear seat of a Super Cub and flown into the base camp—at a cost of $200. At that point, though, he was just glad to get there.

As Perry got his gear from the plane, the guide walked up and introduced himself. In almost the same breath, he asked for the cashier's check for the balance of the hunt cost. As they walked over to the tent camp, Perry was shocked at what he saw: a tent shantytown. Stopping at one tent, the guide told Perry this would be his "cabin." Inside were two army cots with badly-stained mattresses. The tent was heated with an oil-burning stove that left an odor of diesel fuel in the tent.

The cook tent was the guide's headquarters, and there Perry learned that he was the only hunter on this hunt. As he ate a bowl of greasy stew, the guide asked about his hunting license. Surprised, Perry told him he had waited until arrival to get it as the guide had suggested. "Oh, I meant to get it in the village when you arrived there," the guide told him. "I'll fly you back there this afternoon in my plane to get it, but I'll have to charge you $250 for this service."

The next seven days were the worst in Perry's life. He was constantly wet and cold from the lack of the right equipment. The guide never left camp; instead, he had a young man, who admitted he had never guided in this area before, to walk with Perry from daylight until dark. Their lunches were light, and they only had creek water to drink with lunch. Breakfast and dinner were always greasy and never enough. Perry got very little sleep, as the fumes in his tent were so bad he had to keep the flaps open, resulting in temperatures colder than his sleeping bag was designed to handle. He saw little bear sign and never saw a bear.

On the way home, there were several delays in flights, which required him to stay overnight both at the village and in Anchorage and cost him a lot more than he had ever expected. Perry returned home dejected, broke and almost a physical wreck. It would take him a long time to get over his hunt.

This is a true story. The names were changed for obvious reasons. The secret to any hunt, especially hunts for big bear, is to put in a lot of time and careful thought planning the hunt. There is much to consider as you put the hunt together, and *the success or failure of the hunt can be determined by your planning.*

Start Early

Bear hunts cannot be thrown together within a month or two. First of all, bear guides with good reputations for running top-notch hunts are often booked up a year or more in advance. As I was writing this chapter, I talked with Cy Ford, a British Columbia guide with whom I have hunted. He was booked *two years* in advance. Secondly, there are so many things to consider when planning the bear hunt that a great deal of time is needed. It is best to start two years in advance.

The cost of a bear hunt can increase dramatically if you must charter a bush plane.

Which Bear?

The logical starting point when planning a big bear hunt is determining which of the big bear you want to hunt—polar, grizzly or brown. The polar bear is a much-desired trophy for all of us who enjoy bear hunting, but at this writing, polar bear hunting is very limited. The Marine Mammal Protection Act of 1972 prohibits polar bear hunting in Alaska and prohibits U.S. citizens hunting polar bear elsewhere from bringing back the skins. In North America, this leaves only Canada in which to hunt polar bear, and Americans who have a successful hunt must leave their trophies up there.

Canada's polar bear population has been estimated at around 19,000 animals. Hunting is tightly controlled on a quota basis. Eskimos exercise their rights as natives to take about 600 of the allotted harvest for personal use, leaving the sport hunting quota at about 70 animals each year.

Jerome Knap of Canada North Outfitting conducts 45 to 50 polar bear hunts a year around the coast of the Baffin Island, Southampton Island, southern Ellesmere Island, northern Victoria Island and Lancaster Sound. Knap, having hunted over much of the world himself, considers the polar bear hunt the greatest hunting adventure available today. It means going out on the polar ice, living there in igloos or tents with Eskimo guides, and meeting with the bear on its own terms. By international law, polar bear hunts today have to be conducted by traditional means, with dog sleds being the only mode of transportation the hunter can use.

Knap cautions that the polar bear hunter has to face brutal elements. Temperatures are usually well below zero day and night. Blizzards, fog and "white-outs" of frozen ice crystals can occur. At times, polar bear are found only near the floe edge—where sea ice and open water meet. Hunting here has to be very cautious because the ice frequently moves. The guides must be thoroughly experienced in traveling in these types of elements, says Knap.

"Going on a polar bear hunt is like going on a minor Arctic expedition before the age of aircraft," says Knap. The hunter and his guide must be equipped for virtually every emergency the terrain and elements may throw at them. Canada North Outfitting's guides pack food for at least 20 days in case they become stuck in a blizzard. Two-way radios with insulated battery packs are also carried in case of emergency.

A polar bear is nearly always on the move—hunting. An adult bear can trot all day, easily covering 60 miles a day. Knap says the

For a select few, a polar bear hunt is the greatest hunting adventure available today. Temperatures are almost always below zero, transportation is by dog sled and nights are spent in an igloo or four-season tent. There is a two-year waiting list for a polar bear hunt, which costs about $13,500 U.S.

highly mobile nature of the animal makes it even more difficult to hunt. However, the success rate on Knap's polar bear hunts is high—about 90 percent. "But that's because the Canada North Outfitting guides are willing to work hard, sometimes from dawn to dusk," says Knap.

There are two periods when it is possible to hunt polar bear: in early winter from late October to early November, and the main hunting season from mid-March to late May. Before late October, the sea ice is not firm enough to support dog teams and sleds. By late November, the fury of winter has set in and there is almost total darkness.

Bear hunting begins again in March as daylight hours lengthen and the temperatures become more moderate. Then bear start to move about and hunt seals. After late May, the snow may become too soft for the sled. Also, by late May, the bear start to lose their long winter coats and the skins are no longer in their best condition. The legal polar bear season ends May 31.

At this writing, the cost of a polar bear hunt with Canada North Outfitting is $13,500 U.S. and there is a two-year waiting list.

The brown bear—also known as the coastal grizzly or Kodiak bear, whichever you prefer—is popular for those who want a very large bear for their trophy room. Hunting this bear is done along the coast of southern Alaska in a land that is waterlogged and thickly covered with vegetation. These hunts can be physically and mentally demanding, especially if hunting on foot. On brown bear hunts I have spent hours walking through thick alders where vision was limited to 10 feet or less. On the same hunt, I have spent other days wading rushing streams to get up mountain sides where the big bear were feeding.

Other hunts with guides who use boats as their principal means of transportation can be much less demanding. Guides for coastal bear are usually booked a year in advance, and at this writing, hunts are going for an average of $8,000.

Based on a survey I conducted among outfitters, success rates average around 80 percent. The interior grizzly is a trophy of a lifetime, and quite often they are much more aggressive than their larger cousin, the brown bear. Hunting for the grizzly may be conducted in many ways. Days are often spent sitting on a high point glassing valleys and mountain slopes. During some spring hunts, you may spend long days traveling on snowshoes or floating icy rivers in an inflatable boat. Most fall grizzly hunts are part of a combination hunt for moose, caribou and/or Dall sheep.

Along the coast, bear hunting may involve the use of boats. This type of hunt can, at times, be less physically demanding than an inland hunt.

Grizzly hunts are generally a little less expensive than brown bear hunts if grizzly is the only species hunted. At this writing, hunts range from about $4,000 to $8,000. Hunter success on grizzlies varies from guide to guide, with a spring season success average of around 75 percent and a fall season average of about 50 percent. I think in any season a 50 percent success rate is what hunters should expect.

Which of these three bear you elect to hunt is up to your desires, how much you care to spend, your physical and mental ability and whether or not, in the case of the polar bear, you want to earn a trophy that you must leave in Canada.

Spring Or Fall?

Once you've decided on which bear you want to hunt, the next question to answer is whether you want to hunt in the spring or fall. In the case of the polar bear, you have no choice; you go when you can get a hunt. Grizzly and brown bear hunters often prefer the spring season so they can find an animal whose pelt is not rubbed. While spring bear seem to have the better pelts, I have seen bear fresh out of the wintering den that had bad rubs. In areas where snow is on the ground in the spring and hunters can travel on snowshoes, the spring season can be best for the hunter who is in good shape and is willing to work hard for his bear. A good example of this type of hunting is that of Alaska guide Bob Hannon. On his spring grizzly hunts out of Koyuk on the Seward Peninsula, most of his hunters who are in good shape and willing to hunt hard on snowshoes fill their tags.

On the other hand, weather can play a major role in determining when is the best time to hunt during the spring. It is very easy to be a week too early and not see a bear. If you're a week too late, the insects will eat you up and the bear you see may be rubbed.

Where bear are feeding on salmon, the fall hunt is the preference of many hunters simply because the bear are concentrated along streams. Some guides who hunt moose like to have grizzly hunters during the fall, as they can hunt "moose kills" which attract bear. When you are hunting grizzlies as part of a combination hunt, the guide will often hunt the other species first, taking a grizzly if and when spotted while looking for other game.

There are good and bad points associated with both spring and fall bear hunts, and the individual must decide which points are the

Bear hunting usually includes long hours spent glassing valleys and slopes.

most important to him. I personally don't have a preference. I have hunted both seasons successfully, and bad weather has ruined hunts for me during both seasons. As with all hunting, we also need some luck to go along with our skillfully-made decisions. When you can take off work for two weeks may have a lot to do with your decision, as well as the advice of the guide you choose to work with.

Best Areas

One of the questions most often asked by prospective bear hunters is, "Where are the best areas to hunt bear?" I think what they mean to ask is, "Where are bear most numerous?" To answer that question, we must understand a couple of facts.

First, big bear are wanderers. They like to be alone, and an area that may have several bear in it today may not contain a single bear tomorrow.

Secondly, the first-time hunter to the Far North must know that this vast country is not wall-to-wall bear or any other critters. I think the greatest shock I had when I first started working in the Far North country was that large expanses of land are void of game animals during periods of the year. Vast herds of caribou aren't found in every valley, nor is there a bear in every alder thicket. In conjunction with perhaps no other species of game is the word "hunting" more aptly used than in bear hunting.

Many other factors make picking out hot spots for bear hunting difficult. Some areas are closed to bear hunting on relatively short notice, and others are restricted to residents only or are only open in some years. In some areas, such human activity as timber cutting and mining cause the bear population to move on. It is for all these reasons that bear hunters should get a good guide and depend on him to sort out the movement of bear, whims of bureaucrats and impact of "progress."

In order to evaluate the overall big bear situation in North America, let's take a look at each political subdivision and the current bear situation there:

Montana. This is the only state in the lower 48 that permits grizzly hunting, and their population is only a few hundred bear. Hunting there is limited by a quota system; in 1987, the mortality quota was only 14, of which no more than six could be female. This quota includes bear killed by any means. Needless to say, this is not a choice area for the hunter who is wanting a good chance for a grizzly.

Guide Mike Barthelmess of Pine Hills Outfitters in Lincoln, Montana, with one of the few grizzlies taken in Montana during the late 1980s.

Alaska. The Alaska Department of Fish and Game does not differentiate between interior grizzlies and coastal brown bear; they are all brown bear. In 1987, the population of brown bear there was estimated at 32,000 to 43,000 bear. The total kill for 1987 was 1,212 browns, with the three top game management units being unit 9, the Alaska Peninsula area (190 bear); unit 8, the Kodiak Archipelago (169 bear); and unit 13, the area north of Valdez (140 bear). There is no doubt that Alaska gives the best opportunity for bear hunting in North America.

Polar bear hunting is closed in Alaska, and while the possibility of an open season is being discussed, it appears to be years away, if ever.

British Columbia. This is the second-best bet for a grizzly, as the estimated grizzly population in British Columbia is 5,000 to 8,000 bear. Most of the coast and northern mountains of British Columbia offer good hunting. The harvest is on a tightly controlled quota system, which has done a lot to improve the grizzly situation.

Yukon Territory. The Yukon has an estimated grizzly population of between 6,000 and 7,000 bear, which are widely scattered throughout the territory. On average, 85 grizzlies are taken each year by hunters. Guided, non-resident hunters account for most of this harvest, taking about 50 bear each year. Much of the Yukon Territory is not an especially good area for a bear-only hunt. It is, however, a good idea to have a grizzly tag if you are hunting other big game species, as this is when you are most likely to encounter one.

Northwest Territories. Grizzlies are found in about 75 percent of the Northwest Territories, excluding the dense forests of the south. Provincial grizzly biologists have no estimate of the number of grizzlies there because of the vastness of the province and the fact that much of it is uninhabited. For some time this huge area, which comprises roughly one-third of Canada, was closed to non-resident bear hunters. That is changing, as natives of several communities are beginning to guide sport hunters rather than take their quota of bear for subsistence use. The number of bear tags issued to non-resident sport hunters is limited to a small quota, however.

This is the only area in North America open to polar bear hunting, so it is the best.

Alberta. Grizzly bear number only about 800 in Alberta, so the harvest is very limited and open to residents only. According to the Alberta Fish and Wildlife Division, the 1987 grizzly harvest was 43 bear.

Specific Areas To Hunt

As a general rule, there are some areas which are considered especially good at this writing, and with a twinge of reluctance, I will mention them. However, keep in mind, as I have pointed out several times in this book, that browns, grizzlies and polar bear are lone wanderers and there are no permanent hot spots.

For big-bodied browns, the central and southern sections of the Alaskan Peninsula are good. For record-book browns, the Kodiak Archipelago, which includes Kodiak, Raspberry and Afognak Islands, is your best bet. On Kodiak Island alone there are between 2,000 and 3,000 brown bear. Between 1961 and 1987, 148 brown bear that made the Boone & Crockett record book were taken in this area.

The best bets for grizzlies are in British Columbia and Alaska. In British Columbia, the coastal areas around Bella Coola and

Your success on a bear hunt will depend a great deal on your selection of a competent guide. For a listing of NAHC approved big bear guides, see Appendix A.

Kemano are tops, as are the Cassiar Mountains in the northcentral part of the province. In Alaska, the Cooper River area, Seward Peninsula, the headwaters of the Kuskokwim River and some parts of the Brooks Range are considered very good.

Selecting A Guide

Once you have decided which bear you want to hunt, the time of the year, the state or province, whether to use rifle, pistol or bow, the amount of money you can spend, and if you want to hunt other big game or not, it is time to start looking for a guide. This may be a time-consuming part of the planning process, but it is critical to your success that it be done with care.

Unlike most other big game animals, except sheep, to hunt the big bear you are required by law to have a guide unless you are a resident of the state or province. Since this means most of us, we won't discuss do-it-yourself hunts or drop-camp hunting. We have to employ a guide, and it behooves us to get the best one we can for our hunt.

Members of the North American Hunting Club are blessed with a member magazine, *North American Hunter,* which publishes hunting reports on guides that club members have used on hunts. These reports give the name and address of the guide, and the member rates the guide on such things as hunting services and accommodations.

The North American Hunting Club also has available to its members a booklet called "NAHC Approved Outfitters and Guides." It lists guides and outfitters in the U.S. and Canada who have been approved by the majority of the club members hunting with them. These two club services are a good place to start getting names of guides to contact.

The next best source is friends who have hunted with guides. Many of the best bear guides run small operations, and thanks to their success and efforts to run a good service, need little or no advertising. Word of mouth from satisfied clients keeps them booked well in advance. These guides can be selective in the clientele they accept, and they may check you out as well as you check them out.

Hunting shows, such as the NAHC Jamboree and the one put on by Safari Club International, attract guides who have booths or displays on their hunts. By attending one of these events, you can meet a number of guides face-to-face.

One of the less desirable places to select a guide is out of the "guides and outfitters" section of outdoor magazines. You must keep in mind that anyone with enough money can run an enticing ad. Some of the worst guides I've hunted with ran the most alluring ads.

Once you select a list of bear hunting guides you are interested in, write to each of them for their literature. This will give you a little more information to study about each outfit and help you ask specific questions when you go to the next step of the selection process, which is a phone conversation with each guide. Keep in mind when calling guides that most of them spend a good portion of their time in various hunting or fishing camps or running traplines. They are seldom readily available to come to the phone when you call, so you may have to try again and again. If you leave a message, don't be discouraged if you don't get a return call for a few days or even a few weeks. It may be weeks before the guide is back to his home or office to get phone messages.

The best way to go about a phone interview with guides is to write up a questionnaire on each one. This way you will not omit some important question, and after all the interviews are complete, you can compare the answers.

Begin your interview by introducing yourself and telling where you are from. Tell the guide which bear you want to hunt and which hunting season you have in mind. If you want to hunt other big game species, you should tell him that at this time. You should make it clear to him up front if you plan to hunt with a handgun, muzzleloader or bow; it may save both of you some time if he only takes modern rifle hunters.

If you have any physical limitations that would require you to hunt a specific technique, such as by boat or from a blind, you should let him know that early in the conversation. The more he knows about you, the better he can inform you about the services he can or cannot offer.

Once he knows something about you and what you expect, it's time for you to start asking questions, lots of questions. Here are some of the questions you should seek answers to:

1) Where exactly does he bear hunt?
2) What is the terrain like in that area(s)?
3) What is the weather usually like during the time you want to hunt?
4) What hunting techniques are used for bear?
5) Will he or someone else guide you? What is their experience?
6) How long has he been guiding bear hunters? In the area(s) mentioned?
7) How many hunters does he take at one time?
8) What is the camp like? Base camp? Spike camp?
9) What is the guide-to-hunter ratio?
10) How many actual hunting days are included?
11) How do you get to spike camps? (You can't fly and hunt the same day.)
12) What is the cost of this hunt? *Exactly* what does that cover?
13) What about transportation between the airport and base

camp? Who arranges it and is there an additional charge?

14) Is there an additional cost for preparing a trophy for the trip home?

15) Are there any additional expenses? Ask this question at least twice.

16) When does he consider the best time to hunt bear there? Are there openings then?

17) What are the sizes of the bear taken there? Ask both pelt and skull size.

18) What equipment is the hunter expected to furnish?

19) Ask for the names and addresses of two hunters who hunted with him last year and were successful, then two who were not successful.

20) What was his hunter success rate on bear last year? The last five years? I like to save this question for last so I can discuss it at length if necessary and compare it to the discussion which has already taken place. Hunter success will often tell you a lot about a guide. If he tries to fudge on this vital statistic, you'd better watch him. I have had guides tell me they had an 80 percent success rate. When the truth came out that was for all species of big game; bear was only 20 percent. Some—thank goodness they don't usually stay in business long—will tell you whatever they think you want to hear. I like specifics, such as how many bear hunters he had last year and how many actually got a bear. Most guides will be honest with you on this, but there are always a few bad apples in the barrel.

Remember the first guide that Bob Perry called at the beginning of this chapter, the one that Perry thought was trying to talk him out of booking a hunt? He was probably Perry's best bet. When a guide will point out to you the negative points of the hunt as that one did, he's probably being honest, and his candor is definitely a mark in his favor.

Thank the guide for his time and tell him you will get back to him after you check out his references. Next, call the references, including any NAHC members who may have hunted with him. Again, be well organized with written questions.

After introducing yourself and asking permission to discuss their hunt with XYZ guide service, begin asking these questions:

1) How would they rate their overall hunt?

2) Were they successful? If so, what was the size of the bear and distance of the shot?

3) How many hunters were in base camp? Spike camp?
4) How was the food? Lodging? Guide's equipment?
5) Was there enough help in camp?
6) Was the hunt well organized?
7) Who was their guide? How would they rate him?
8) What hunting technique was used?
9) What form of transportation was used to spike camps? To and from the airport?
10) Were there any hidden costs?
11) What was the weather like? The terrain?
12) How many bear did they see?
13) What did they not like about the hunt?
14) Did the guide do a good job with the pelt and skull?
15) Would they hunt with him again?
16) What equipment did they not have that they wish they had taken?

By the time you have the answers to these questions from four different people, you will most likely have a good idea about the guide and his operation. Now you must decide whether or not you want to bet several thousand dollars on him.

Assuming you decide to go with him, you should call right away to let him know your decision and discuss dates and costs in detail. Be sure to find out what his deposit and cancellation policies are. This is especially true when planning a year or more in advance. Request a contract spelling out the details of your transaction, including cancellation policy, deposit and final payment information. While you are on the phone with him, ask what calibers and loads he prefers. Also, request a detailed what-to-bring list so that you can begin to gather the needed gear.

When you hang up, you should immediately send him a letter spelling out your understanding of your arrival and departure dates from his camp, total cost, deposit and final payment, including when and how payment will be made (usually upon arrival by cashier's check) and cancellation agreement. This will let him see in writing what you understand the deal to be, and if there is any misunderstanding, you can get it straightened out quickly.

If you book a hunt a year or more in advance, you should talk to the guide every few months just to stay in touch. Guides, like all businessmen, go bankrupt, lose their territory, die, get ill, etc., and you should look after your deposit. In addition, you get to know him better and keep up with his hunting success.

You may find it difficult to book the guide you really wanted, as he has filled up his hunts. If so, try to get on his waiting list. When I was in the hunting business, I had cancellations every year and maintained a waiting list to fill those openings.

Know All Costs

An important step in the planning process is to determine as much of the cost of your bear hunt as you can. Many hunters inexperienced at hunting the Far North mentally accept the $8,000 or so cost of booking the hunt to be about all of the cost. This can be a trap.

In addition to the cost of the hunt, expect necessary hunting licenses to be another $400 or more. Round-trip commercial air fare, depending on where you're flying from, might be another $800-plus. There could be an air taxi or charter flight cost, ranging between $200 and $500 each way for transportation to the guide's camp.

More often than not, the remoteness of Far North hunting camps means traveling at least one day in advance of and after your hunt. Accommodations and meals for those days might run another $300 or more. It is not at all uncommon to be weathered in along the route, which can cost as much as $200 per day for room and meals. I have spent as long as five days waiting in some small village for the weather to break, paying top dollar for a tiny room and overcooked hamburgers. Local cab fares are often outrageous, but you have no choice. This delay wasn't in the hunting plans at all.

If you are successful on the hunt, there may be an extra charge for the additional baggage (skin and skull) on your return trip. This could amount to $50 or more. If you took advantage of a special booking price on your commercial airline tickets that imposes a penalty for making schedule changes, a delay in getting out of camp because of weather can mean some stiff additional charges.

Several years ago, my wife and I had been hunting in a bear camp in British Columbia for two weeks. Our hunt was successful, and we came out of the bush right on time to stay with our flight schedule. At the little airport where we were to catch our commercial flight, we learned that United Airlines, with which our return flights were booked, was crippled by a pilots' strike. To make a long story short, it took us three days to get home at an enormous cost we hadn't expected.

Looking at what can and often does happen, you can see that the $8,000 grizzly hunt in reality costs $10,000 to $12,000. Not all hunts, thank goodness, run into all these problems and extra cost, but it happens often enough that you should look for the hidden costs in your planning and carry some extra travelers' checks with you. Don't depend on credit cards; I've been in some remote settlements where charter services, hotels and restaurants didn't accept credit cards.

While a lot of these costs can't be planned for, such as getting weathered in along the way, some thoughtful planning can cut your surprises down to a minimum.

Get all the hunt license information from your guide in advance. Find out if you need a general and/or big game non-resident license in addition to a polar, brown or grizzly license. Ask what, if any, special permits are required. Find out the total cost of all necessary licenses, permits, etc. When should you get them and where? Be sure you have a clear understanding of where. Standing in the middle of an air strip at base camp is the wrong time to find out that the nearest hunting license vendor is 150 miles away. Don't assume anything. Your guide should be able to provide all this information.

As mentioned earlier, press your guide to tell you exactly what services his fee does and does not include and the costs of additional services. Some guides charge extra for preparing trophies to be flown out. There may also be other additional charges, such as for additional days in camp due to getting weathered in. Your contract should spell all this out.

Another expense that is entirely optional but frequently included is a tip for your guide and/or other camp personnel. Since it is not obligatory, the amount of any tip you want to give is also up to you. However, a common amount given to a guide who has done a good job and helped you get a trophy is $100. Even if your hunt has not been successful but you feel that the guide has given exceptional effort, a $50 to $100 tip would not be unusual.

Other camp personnel who are frequently tipped include wranglers who have been helpful to you, base camp cooks who prepare good meals, camp hands who might flesh and care for your bear skins, and anyone else whose special effort you would like to reward. A common amount for these people is $20 to $30.

It has been my experience as both a guide/outfitter and big game hunter that the owner of the guiding service is not usually tipped, even if he is the one who guides you. Hunters do frequently give gifts, such as outdoor equipment, to the owner/guide, either while they are there or by mail after the hunt. It is not at all uncommon for hunters to leave a piece of equipment that they used on the hunt, such as a hunting knife, binoculars or extra ammunition, with the owner/guide, especially in the Far North where equipment is harder to come by.

Be sure to check with your travel agent concerning extra cost for additional baggage in the event you are returning with a big bear pelt and skull. Also know and understand your options if you don't make your return schedule on time.

After getting into several uncomfortable situations due to unplanned, unexpected costs on Far North hunting trips, I now make it a policy to carry an additional $1,500 in travelers' checks and $500 U.S. or Canadian cash, depending on where I'm going, to meet these unforeseen eventualities. This is in addition to what I think I will need. It has come in handy several times.

Another precaution I now take is to get the name, address and phone number of someone the guide knows in the town or village I fly into nearest his camp. In the event I am suddenly stuck in a remote village which is not really equipped for tourists, I have someone who will give me a hand getting my problems solved. Also, if he likes you, it can sometimes save you a lot of money on room cost, meals, ground transportation and other expenses.

Some hunters I know send their firearms and hunting gear by air freight, insured, up to their guide a week or two early to make sure it's there when they arrive. I, like many other hunters, have had to borrow clothes and a gun on a hunt because my luggage didn't arrive when I did. The mishandling of luggage is common now, and it is good to work out a plan with your guide to have it sent up early.

Planning a bear hunt is a big undertaking, but one that is necessary to protect your investment and give you a reasonable chance for success. As the story at the beginning of this chapter demonstrated, poor planning can spell grief and even disaster when you're hunting big bear.

1961-1987
Alaska Brown/Grizzly Sport Harvest
By Game Management Unit

Unit Number	Total Bear Harvested
1	443
2	0
3	2
4	2,009
5	537
6	904
7	34
8	3,787
9	5,146
10	136
11	349
12	511
13	1,810
14	210
15	162
16	948
17	671
18	133
19	877
20	998
21	94
22	429
23	667
24	297
25	419
26	438

When planning your big bear hunt in Alaska, be sure to investigate the success of past hunters in your prospective game management unit.

1961-1987
Alaska Sport Harvest—Brown/Grizzly Bear

Year	Total
1961	471
1962	536
1963	557
1964	636
1965	782
1966	866
1967	791
1968	644
1969	512
1970	632
1971	740
1972	834
1973	926
1974	779
1975	827
1976	832
1977	774
1978	819
1979	883
1980	882
1981	887
1982	823
1983	973
1984	1,118
1985	1,156
1986	1,119
1987	1,212

The Alaska sport harvest of brown and grizzly bear has continued to climb at an impressive rate.

4

Conditioning
For The Hunt

Conditioning the body and the mind for the hunt cannot be over-emphasized. Regardless of how well the bear hunter can shoot, how good his guide may be or how many bear are in an area, if the hunter is not in good—and I mean *very good*—physical and mental condition, his chances for success are slim. When I surveyed guides throughout big bear country, the most common reason they gave for bear hunters not being successful was the hunters not being in good physical or mental condition for the hunt.

Contrary to popular opinion, big bear hunting is not easy. In fact, the polar bear hunt by dog sled is generally considered the most demanding hunt in North America. Grizzly and brown bear hunting run a close second, being on par with sheep hunting.

When you embark on long days of walking on soggy ground wearing hip boots, days in deep snow wearing snowshoes, climbing steep mountains and crossing roaring streams, often carrying your camp on your back, you had better be in good condition. Your guide, who will be in shape, will want to work hard to get you a bear, but he can't do his job effectively if you can't keep up.

I have been on many hunts where a hunter who thought he was in good shape would give up the hunt after two or three days. I once saw an entire group of five hunters call their hunt off after only two days of hunting. They hadn't gotten off to a good start when blisters, obesity and lack of endurance did them in. Two other hunters, both in good shape, working out of the same base camp took near-record book bear by the sixth day and saw a total of seven bear.

Because bear are wanderers, it takes a lot of searching to find one, and in most cases, that means a lot of walking. That requires strong legs, not only for going up hills, but perhaps more importantly, for coming down steep hills. Due to the likelihood of carrying a backpack or a day pack, wearing lots of clothes, pulling yourself up steep slopes, fighting alders, etc., the upper body should be strong and in peak shape.

Your physical condition should have a lot to do with which guide you choose, based on the hunting technique he employs. If you feel that long hard walks over steep terrain are out, you may want to opt for a guide who uses horses or boats for transportation. However, if you don't normally ride horses, that activity can be rough on the body. Using a boat for spotting is often the least physically demanding of the hunting techniques.

The best way to prepare physically is to begin getting your body in shape for the bear hunt months before the hunt date. There are literally hundreds of work-out programs in print that are supposed to put your body back in shape, but the best program I've ever tried was developed by North American Hunting Club member Dennis Campbell. Campbell is a pharmacist who devotes a lot of time each year to hunting big game throughout North America. He is an official measurer for the Boone & Crockett Club and for Safari Club International.

Early in his big-game hunting career, Campbell noticed that the various conditioning programs he tried didn't really prepare him for the rigors of his hunts. He also noticed that his positive mental attitude toward the hunt was directly related to the condition of his body for each hunt. Because of his dissatisfaction with existing conditioning programs, Campbell set out to develop his own, utilizing his formal education in pharmacy and his background as a college athlete.

His goal was a fitness program that was simple and flexible, yet prepared him for bear, sheep, goat or any other type of hunting which might involve lots of difficult walking, climbing, backpacking and horseback riding. After several years of trial and error, he finally came up with a conditioning program that is simple, yet provides him outstanding results. I have also followed this routine

NAHC member Dennis Campbell (above) developed a conditioning program specifically for hunters. The author believes that it is the most comprehensive and effective conditioning program available today. The program includes jumping rope, which increases muscular strength and tone, and improves stamina and breathing.

and can attest to its effectiveness. While Campbell's program might not be right for you, you might find it useful in planning your own.

The first step before you begin any conditioning program is to get a good physical from your doctor and be sure it includes a stress EKG. Explain to your doctor in detail your hunting plans and get his approval of the conditioning program you have selected to get ready for that hunt.

Campbell's conditioning program consists of four basic exercises and two occasional or substitute exercises. The four basic ones are jumping rope, pushups, bicycling and walking. The occasional exercises are climbing stairs and jogging.

Campbell considers jumping rope the most beneficial activity in a hunter's conditioning program, as the benefits are numerous. It increases the strength and tone of the hips, stomach, thighs and calves and improves breathing and stamina. You should use a good-quality jump rope with ballbearing handles made of leather.

Campbell feels there is no substitute for pushups, even if you have to begin by doing pushups on your hands and knees, gradually increasing your strength to do a traditional pushup. The benefit of the pushup is to increase your upper body strength. You must be strong in the upper body for a horseback or backpack hunt.

Bicycling is a great exercise for building up thigh muscles used for going up and down steep hills. Campbell uses an exercise bike with a pressure-adjustable wheel, speedometer and odometer.

He considers walking better than jogging, since it does not cause stress to the skeletal system, kidneys and other organs. If you will be taking a backpack hunt, you should walk with a loaded backpack. The extra weight will add the desired strength with less distance required. Also, wear your hunting boots when walking, as this conditions the feet to the boot and breaks in boots before the hunt.

Climbing stairs is Campbell's exercise of choice for an occasional break in the routine, and he recommends it to those who cannot master rope jumping.

Jogging is a substitute for walking for those who already jog.

When to begin your exercise program is of great importance. Campbell begins as far as six months in advance of the hunt, but three months will generally be sufficient unless you are very overweight. If you are overweight, you should begin dieting six months or more in advance, depending upon the amount of weight to be lost.

Bicycling develops the thigh muscles to enable the hunter to climb steep hills, which are common in big bear country.

Start your conditioning program very slowly, especially if you are overweight or have a medical condition that warrants extra caution. Depending on your present condition, begin with something you can actually handle, then each week add more repetitions of the exercises you are using. Most people agree that an every-other-day workout is a good program.

Warnings And Tips

Do not work up at too fast a pace. If you move ahead more than you should have, drop back to your previous level.

If you miss a workout or two, don't get discouraged; just start back where you left off.

Divide and space your pushups before, between and after the jumps.

Wear good-quality jogging shoes when jumping rope. This will save your feet, ankles and shins a lot of wear and tear.

Campbell recommends that you begin walking or hiking on the off days starting a month after the every-other-day program. Begin slowly on this also. One mile a day for the first couple of weeks should be sufficient. Increase as you feel you can, and don't forget to wear your hunting boots.

Mix in the climbing stairs and/or jogging as you desire and according to your schedule. If you work in or near a building with several flights of stairs, you will have the perfect opportunity before or after work.

Campbell's Program

Here is Campbell's 12-week conditioning program. You may need to begin at a different level and increase at a faster or slower pace, according to your ability and physical condition. Twelve weeks is generally ample time to get into shape.

Week 1: 100 rope jumps; 15 pushups (five before jumping rope, five after each 50 jumps); one-half mile on the bicycle.

Week 2: 150 rope jumps; 20 pushups (five before jumping rope, five after each 50 jumps); one mile on the bicycle.

Week 3: 200 rope jumps; 25 pushups; one mile on the bicycle.

Week 4: 250 rope jumps; 30 pushups; two miles on the bicycle.

Walking in hiking boots while wearing a loaded backpack is an important part of the conditioning process.

Week 5: 300 rope jumps; 35 pushups; two miles on the bicycle. Add a one-mile walk on off days.

Week 6: 350 rope jumps; 40 pushups; three miles on the bicycle; one-mile walk every other day.

Week 7: 400 rope jumps; 45 pushups; three miles on the bicycle; one-mile walk with backpack every other day.

Week 8: 450 rope jumps; 50 pushups; three miles on the bicycle; one-mile walk with backpack every other day.

Week 9: 500 rope jumps; 55 pushups; three miles on the bicycle; one mile walk with pack every other day.

Week 10: 550 rope jumps; 60 pushups; three miles on the bicycle; two-mile walk with pack every other day.

Week 11: 600 rope jumps; 65 pushups; four miles on the bicycle; two-mile walk with pack every other day.

Week 12: 650 rope jumps; 70 pushups; four miles on the bicycle; two- or three-mile walk with pack every other day.

If you can follow this conditioning program or a similar one, you will be ready for any hunt you would like to take, including a difficult bear hunt. Of course, any extra exercise you could add to the program would mean an even better physical condition.

Mental Conditioning

Closely associated to physical conditioning for a bear hunt is mental conditioning, or developing the ability to maintain a positive mental attitude throughout the entire hunt. I have seen many big, strong, in-shape hunters give up on a hard hunt long before the hunt was over. Regardless of how good their guide was, it was difficult to put them on a trophy. They weren't willing to hunt hard and were not confident in themselves or their guide. This can be downright dangerous when hunting big bear.

Generally speaking, most hunters, when in good physical condition, are also mentally ready for a hard hunt. But due to personalities, there are some whose bodies are positive but minds are negative. The morale of everyone in camp can be diminished

Bear hunting takes place in a land that is vast and full of dangers, such as this glacial crevasse.

Don't go on a bear hunt expecting to see lots of bear; chances are good that you won't. Be prepared to hunt just as hard the last day with the enthusiasm you had on the first day. This brings success.

by one hunter with a negative attitude who complains constantly about the weather, the food, the number or size of the bear seen, etc. Unfortunately, some hunters think they should see bear every day and fill their tags on the first day or two. Look at it this way: if you were reasonably expected to kill a bear so soon, why would the guide have booked you for a 10- to 14-day hunt? If you're going to be complaining and ready to come home after the third day just because you haven't seen bear yet, you should save your money and stay home.

Then there's the hunter who is not up to the hunt physically. He will often develop a negative mental attitude early in the hunt. He is embarrassed by not being able to keep up the pace, he feels bad all the time, and he may feel guilty for having spent the family's vacation money for a hunt he's not up to.

Other reasons I have noticed that put hunters in a negative frame of mind include the vastness of the wilderness in which bear hunting is conducted. It's one thing to see vast, open tundra or thick, alder-covered slopes on television, but something quite different when you are there for the first time. The harsh weather that goes along with a hunt in the Far North often frightens hunters. The primitive living conditions in some base or spike camps causes many modern hunters to feel negatively toward the guide and lose confidence in the hunt. I have seen this happen even in very comfortable camps. To some people, camping is fun until you do it.

The days of anticipation associated with hunting an animal that is potentially dangerous can take its toll on many hunters. They constantly expect a grizzly to come charging out of every alder thicket or into their tent every night. Each day they become more keyed up until they are about to explode. To escape this feeling, they want to stay in the safety of camp, or if they get a chance to shoot, they will forget marksmanship and shot placement, electing to point and pull the trigger just to get it over with.

From time to time there is a bear hunter who totally loses his mental control, usually when very close to a bear, and cannot fire his rifle. I have never witnessed this myself, but I have talked to guides who have. Darwin Watson of Christina Falls Outfitters in British Columbia related such a story to me.

During the 1987 hunting season, Watson took one of his hunters into a spike camp to hunt grizzlies. After a four-hour horseback ride in the rain, they set up camp and proceeded to look for a moose kill where one of Watson's other guides had successfully gotten a hunter a bull moose. Due to some rather bad directions, Watson and his hunter ended up in some heavily-burned timber, not sure where the moose kill was.

Both men had rifles, and due to the continuing rain, both were completely suited in nylon raingear—not exactly a quiet procession. Their intentions were to find the moose kill and check for grizzly sign. Watson knew they were reasonably close. He came to realize just how close when he heard a growl and spotted a large grizzly on a burned log only eight to 10 paces away. Swinging his rifle up and sighting on the bear's neck, he directed his hunter to shoot. The hunter swung his rifle up and froze. Despite Watson's rather frantic pleadings to shoot, the hunter just stood there for 10 seconds or so with the bear roaring in their faces. Then the bear turned and disappeared.

Watson said the hunter later admitted to being frozen with fright, which, as it turned out, was probably best for all concerned under the circumstances. They did get a similar-looking bear three days later about four miles away.

I have seen several instances where the shooting was anything but good due to fear and/or excitement. This can be a lot worse than freezing and not shooting at all. Having a bear get away without a shot being fired is far better than having a gutshot grizzly on one's hands.

Second only to poor physical condition, the major cause of a hunter developing a negative attitude toward the hunt is the misconception about the abundance of game in the vast Far North. Books, magazines, TV and movies have led many people to believe that the Yukon, British Columbia and Alaska have bear in large numbers everywhere. Nothing could be further from the truth. Bear are most often difficult to find.

It is not unusual to hunt in this vast country for days and not only fail to find bear, but not see any other game animals either. After a few days of this, many hunters think they've been had by their guide. They give up mentally and cease to hunt hard. They forget that the name of their sport is "hunting," and that means right up until the last moment.

I can't count how many really good bear I've heard about that were taken on the last day of a 10- or 14-day hunt. In many cases, it was the only bear seen. Don't go on a bear hunt expecting to see lots of bear; chances are good that you won't. Be prepared to hunt just as hard the last day with the enthusiasm you had on the first day. This brings about success.

A bear hunt is tough and usually physically demanding beyond your expectations. The weather can be rotten for days. The days are long and the nights short. The camps can be somewhat primitive, and the land is vast and can be hostile.

Big bear are hard to find and may be few in number. The chances are greater that you will get your bear in the last day of the hunt than on the first day. These hunts are expensive, but you may go home without a bear. If you can accept these facts, keeping a positive mental attitude and a high degree of confidence and enthusiasm throughout the hunt, then you will make a good bear hunter. If, being honest with yourself, your personality or disposition clashes with any of these factors, you may want to consider something other than bear hunting.

5

Clothes And Personal Gear For The Bear Hunt

The air was full of excitement. It was the fifth morning of our grizzly hunt, and a cold, wet snow had blown in off the coast to replace the constant rain we had been enduring since we arrived. All four of us had seen grizzlies, and one of our hunters had taken a nice 8-foot 6-inch male.

As we gathered with our guides in the cook tent to plan the day's hunt, one member of our group announced that he had had all the grizzly hunting he wanted and would not be going out. His announcement came as no surprise to me. I had watched Doug fight gear problems ever since we arrived.

Doug was an experienced hunter and an above-average shot on game. He was in good physical condition and the last person you would expect to quit in the middle of a hunt. His problem was that his clothing and personal equipment were ill-chosen and had failed him. Doug was miserable each day in the harsh, wet Alaskan climate, and he finally just gave up.

Doug's problems started the day we arrived. He left the flap of his tent open, and the blowing rain soaked his expensive, down-filled sleeping bag. He had brought a cheap air mattress that had gotten punctured in his duffel bag on the flight up from his home in Ohio. He was getting no sleep at all.

Doug's clothing was not chosen with care. His long underwear was made from 100 percent wool, and after the first long day's walk, Doug was constantly tugging at the underwear and scratching. Even though the guide had done a good job of describing the weather possibilities and terrain, Doug had chosen to wear his "good luck" hunting hat, a western-style broad-brimmed hat, and an old rainsuit he had used for years. The alder thickets we were constantly walking through made ribbons of the worn-out rainsuit, and Doug almost drove his guide crazy going back to retrieve his cowboy hat blown off in the wind.

Since we were hunting in rain, needless to say, Doug was soaked from the beginning. His down-filled jacket looked like a wet horse blanket, and Doug was cold all the time. In spite of the fact that Doug had been told to wear wool trousers for this early spring hunt, he had brought only blue jeans, which stayed wet and clung to his legs, robbing him of warmth.

In short, this hunter was denied a good hunt simply because his clothing and personal gear were ill-chosen and failed him. Everyone on that hunt but Doug got a good bear.

Over the years I have seen Doug's story repeated many times. When you're out in the bush in some of the most unpredictable weather on earth, hunting an animal that can be dangerous, you had better have the right gear. Doug didn't, and he threw away about $10,000, not to mention the best chance he may ever have at taking a good grizzly.

I have been on grizzly hunts where the weather would vary drastically. The sun would break out and it would be hot for a few hours, bringing along with it hordes of mosquitoes. Next, a cold rain would blow in, carried by a 30-mile-per-hour wind. Finally, the wind would die down and snow would fall. I have also been on spring and fall hunts where it would be cold and snowing for most of the hunt.

It is during cold weather that hunters tend to have the most trouble dressing properly. It is also the weather that you are most likely to encounter on a big bear hunt, and failing to dress properly for the cold can mean results much worse than just discomfort. Frostbite and hypothermia are serious threats in the Far North.

The best way to dress for a cold day of bear hunting is by wearing layers of clothing that provide both insulation and ventilation. As opposed to wearing one very heavy garment, wearing several layers of clothing preserves your body heat while allowing body moisture to evaporate freely.

Another benefit of the layering system is that as the weather changes and you become warmer or colder, layers can be removed

Careful attention to your clothing and personal gear will play a major role in determining whether your bear hunt is successful and enjoyable.

Being prepared for harsh weather was one factor that helped handgun hunter Larry Kelly take this big grizzly.

or added. The layering concept has been practiced by outdoorsmen for hundreds of years, but today we have garments that make it perform at its best.

The first layer is the "skin layer"—underwear. Underwear provides next-to-the-skin comfort and should be able to "breathe," allowing moisture to escape. This process of breathing wicks moisture from the skin into the outer layers of clothing. Socks are also part of the skin layer and provide the same function.

The second layer is the inner insulating layer and should be made of loose-fitting layers of shirts, pants, sweaters, vests, boots, and insulated pants. When worn loose, the clothes in this layer can breathe to further expel moisture. On warm, dry days, this could be the final layer.

The third layer is the outer insulating layer, and its job is to protect your body with an insulation that stops the chill of wind and penetrating cold. This layer can also serve as a protective layer, shielding the wearer from rain, snow, briers and brush. This layer is composed of jackets, parkas, hats, gloves, insulated coveralls, etc. This is often the final layer needed.

The fourth layer is the special protective layer. For bear hunting, it may consist of a rainsuit, hip boots or other items to fulfill a special need.

Skin Layer

The layer of clothing that is next to the skin is extremely important, especially in cold weather. During warm, dry weather, cotton or ordinary synthetic underwear and socks will not get you into trouble; however, in weather that is wet and/or cold, as you will generally encounter on big bear hunts, you have a different and often dangerous situation.

When wet, cotton or cotton/polyester underwear loses its insulating value and increases the rate at which the body loses its heat. For many years the outdoorsman's only effective choice of long underwear for cold weather was wool or two-layered underwear made of cotton on the inside and wool on the outside. However, thanks to high-tech breakthroughs in man-made fabrics, today there are some other choices in underwear for wet and/or cold weather that give the wearer maximum protection. The first man-made fabric to enter the underwear market with very positive results was polypropylene. This non-absorbent, soft, stretchable, body-hugging fabric wicks moisture away from the skin, yet it stops the movement of air on the skin's surface, resulting in a retention of body heat.

An effective use of polypropylene is in medium-weight underwear for active outdoorsmen, a two-layered garment that combines 53 percent soft wool with 47 percent polypropylene. The polypropylene is the inner layer and the wool is the outer. This combination allows moisture to be wicked away from the skin to the outer wool layer, where the moisture evaporates. This keeps the layer next to the skin dry, and when you add to that the insulating value of the wool, you have warmth in very cold weather.

One of the most effective underwear fabrics for cold or wet weather is DuPont's Thermax. It is made from a unique hollow fiber which has been designed to give wearers the softness of cotton, but with wicking ability to pull moisture away from the body for evaporation.

The hollow fiber used in the construction of the fabric also maximizes the amount of entrapped air to provide superior insulating capabilities, a critical factor to warmth. Thermax is easy to care for, as it retains its shape and resists shrinkage when laundered. It is also resistant to mildew and doesn't retain odor.

Here are some points to consider when buying underwear for cold weather:

1) Purchase wool, cotton or wool/cotton blend underwear one size larger, as some shrinkage will be experienced when laundering.

2) When selecting two-piece long underwear, be sure the top half is long enough to fit well down into the lower half. Exposed bare skin in the kidney area can chill the wearer and offset the value of the underwear.

3) Don't buy underwear with legs that are too long for you. Long legs may bunch up in the boot, cutting off circulation and resulting in cold feet.

4) Follow the laundering instructions to the letter. Wool can shrink to the point of looking like it was made for a child. Polypropylene, as well as many other synthetics, is sensitive to heat, and excessive heat may ruin its shape.

Socks are an essential part of the skin layer. Like underwear, their comfort and wicking ability plays a major role in keeping the wearer warm.

The part of us that seems to get cold first is the feet, and with good reason. Our body is programmed to automatically regulate its warmth requirements for survival. In cold conditions, the brain and central nervous system receive the highest priority. In order to keep these vital areas warm, circulation to the extremities is curtailed. Since our feet are the furthest from the core, they are the first to feel the reduced circulation. Thus, cold feet.

Cold weather foot covering should start with two pairs of socks. Since the feet are active sweat producers, the socks next to the skin should be made of polypropylene or Thermax for the same reasons they are used as underwear.

The outer socks should be of wool or wool-blend. Don't wear socks that are too thick, as they can cut off circulation when wedged between the foot and a tight-fitting boot. Make sure your wool sock is high enough to come up above the top of the boot. This can keep it from slipping down into the boot and cutting off circulation.

Before you put on your boots, make sure all wrinkles are smoothed out of your socks. Wrinkled socks are not only

The author's inner insulating layer of wool is loose-fitting to permit easy blood circulation. Note the suspenders which allow the trousers to be worn loose.

uncomfortable, but they also slow down the blood circulation to the feet and toes and can cause blisters.

Bear hunters are likely to do a great deal of walking and it will frequently be in wet conditions, so carry an extra pair of liner socks and wool socks in your day pack. Change socks when your feet become damp and cold.

The Inner Insulating Layer

The second layer of clothing is one which the wearer can tailor to fit the circumstances of the hunt. In cool weather, the shirt may be of chamois or corduroy, worn with lightweight cotton duck pants or denim jeans. However, when the weather gets cold, this layer must be taken more seriously.

In cold weather, the upper part of the inner insulating layer must serve several purposes. It must first insulate. Secondly, it must be capable of ventilating. In order to carry out these functions, it is best if several layers are worn. Let's say that on an early-morning, late-spring bear hunt, you know that it's going to be in the low 20s for the first few hours, but later on during the day you expect temperatures in the 40s. Over your underwear you may wear a long-sleeved cotton blend shirt, with a wool sweater over that. If, in fact, the day does warm up, you can pull off the sweater and store it in your day pack.

These layers can be made up of shirts, sweaters and vests. The number and weight are a choice that only you can make based on your own comfort requirements, but there are a few principles to remember. All layers should be from medium to light weight. It is better to have two or three layers than one heavy shirt. These layers should not be so bulky as to make movement difficult. They should fit loosely so that you get a bellows effect to facilitate ventilation when moving around. Shirts should have long tails that will stay inside the trousers, even after a long day of climbing over obstacles, to protect the kidney area.

If cold and wet conditions are expected, a shirt made of wool blend will be a good choice, as wool is not only warm, but resistant to moisture and warm even when wet. Wool breathes, allowing body vapor to evaporate, and is superior in quietness.

The second part of this layer is the pants. First of all, the pants selected should not be too tight around the waist. When trying on pants, remember to leave a little room for long underwear. The belt loops should be wide enough to accommodate your hunting belt. The pants should be cuffless, as cuffs are collection points for sticks, pebbles, snow, etc. Wool and other heavy pants should have buttons for attaching suspenders.

When purchasing hunting pants for bear hunting, keep in mind the conditions under which you will be using them. Will you need wool for snow and damp cold? Will you be hunting in thick brush, briers or rocks, where tough Cordura fabric or nylon-faced pants will be needed? The answers to these questions will help you select the proper hunting pants. Also, your guide can help you make a wise selection.

How you hold your pants up is important during cold weather. A surprising number of people hunting during cold weather have cold feet and legs due, in part, to the fact they have their belt too tight. This restricts circulation, causing the extremities to get cold, and also stops ventilation, which adds to the problem. A good pair of suspenders can go a long way toward keeping you warm. Outdoorsmen in colder climates have known this for centuries.

Even with suspenders, a belt is an important item of equipment, as it is where items such as knife sheaths, cartridge holders and mini-flashlight holders are worn. Belts are also needed if hip boots or brush chaps are worn, as these items are attached to the belt. They should be of good quality and not rolled over around the edges. Elastic belts and narrow ones are inappropriate for hunters.

One of the single most important items in the layering system is included in this layer—footwear. No bear hunter can do his or her best with tired, hurting or cold feet. Since most bear hunting trips include a lot of walking, good footwear is important to the well-being of the hunter and to the enjoyment of the hunt.

It wasn't too long ago that hunting boots were little more than work or military surplus boots in a different box. However, thanks to modern technology and materials, this has changed, and now there are lightweight boots available for hunting that can also keep your feet dry and warm.

In the past, leather was the only quality material of which boots were made. But leather has been joined by man-made materials which provide many of the same advantages. DuPont's Cordura nylon has enabled boot and shoe manufacturers to make rugged footwear that is lightweight. Some boots weigh half as much as they did when they were all leather. Also, boots made with Cordura may come in a camouflage pattern, and they are quick to dry. Cordura is strong and abrasion-resistant. Several boot companies use Cordura and leather as the outer layer of hunting

Waterproof pacs are ideal in wet conditions common in bear country.

boots with a full-sock Gore-Tex inner lining for waterproofing. Thinsulate is also being used as insulation for warmth.

The soles of boots have changed a great deal as well. Several years ago the choices in soles were slim, usually heavy lugged soles or smooth soles. Now there is a wide variety of soles which range in between these extremes. The new soles are lighter and much more flexible.

For bear hunting in rough areas during all types of weather, a waterproof, all-leather or Cordura/leather combination boot 10 to 12 inches high would be a good choice. The type of sole selected should be given some thought and matched to the terrain most likely to be encountered. A deep-treaded sole is excellent for climbing rocky mountains but can add pounds to your feet if worn in a muddy area.

Whether or not to purchase insulated boots is a factor to be considered. If most of your hunting is done during warmer months, then the need for insulation may not be great.

If you elect to purchase some of the high-quality leather boots found on today's market, be sure you learn to care for them properly. Get a good supply of a wax compound such as Sno-Seal and coat the boots regularly according to directions.

For wet conditions, the popular leather or Cordura top and rubber-bottomed "pacs" are often a good choice. Many of these boots are waterproof and may be purchased with insulated liners, which make them good for use in very cold weather and in snow.

If you purchase these boots with a removable insulating liner, be sure to buy an extra liner or two to have along when one gets wet.

Regardless of which type of shoe or boot you select, be sure to take your time in getting fitted. Wear the same sock combination to the store that you plan to wear with the boots in the field. Make sure that the footwear is not too tight with that sock combination. Purchase an extra set of laces when you buy your footwear and keep the laces in your day pack. Be sure to get complete instructions on how to properly care for your new footwear.

When wearing your boots in cold weather, remember not to lace them tightly. This can reduce blood circulation and cause cold feet. Many seasoned hunters buy their cold weather boots one full size larger than normal to comfortably wear two pairs of socks.

The Outer Insulating Layer

The first item to consider for this layer is a cap or hat for the head. During warm weather, a baseball-style cap goes a long way toward keeping the head shaded and cool. However, as the weather cools down, more serious consideration needs to be given to the head gear. A tremendous amount of the body's total heat production may be lost through an unprotected head.

For cool days when hunting in high open country, a beaver-felt, western-style hat will conserve heat and protect the head from bright sun, rain, hail or sleet. In other areas, the hunter may want to wear a Jones-style hat or baseball-style cap that is insulated. Make sure the cap you choose can be pulled down to give your ears protection.

If the weather is cold, many hunters want maximum protection. This is provided by a knit cap called a balaclava, or snow or tundra mask. It can be worn rolled up as a knit cap. When the weather gets colder, it can be rolled down to serve as a face mask, giving protection to the head, face and neck. At one time, the best balaclavas were made of wool and were uncomfortable to many people when worn next to the skin. Now balaclavas are available with a wool outer layer and polypropylene inner layer.

The outer layer of cold-weather clothing consists of warm headgear, such as this balaclava, an insulated coat and insulated gloves.

The polypropylene is comfortable next to the skin and does a good job of wicking moisture away from the head.

When it is windy or raining, the balaclava will not be enough. At this time, an insulated hood on a coat or parka will be needed, or at least a rainsuit with a hood.

If weather is uncertain, a balaclava can be carried in the day pack and a cooler hat worn. Since the head is a principal point of heat loss, when properly covered it can warm other parts of the body. The mountain men had a saying, ''When your feet are cold, put on your hat.'' It makes sense.

The second item in this layer is the coat, jacket, parka or coveralls you will wear. Obviously, if it is warm, you may not need a coat of any type. However, if your hunt takes you into the really cold country where rain or snow is likely, you need to know something about insulation and fabrics.

Insulation does not furnish us with any heat. Our body generates the heat. It is the job of the insulation to hold our body's heat next to us. The best insulation known is dead air. Heat is taken away from the body by the movement of warm air and is replaced by cold air. In order to stay warm, we must stop this movement and circulation of air. Once air is "chopped up" into small pockets and its movement stopped, it is known as dead air, and dead air is what holds in heat. The insulating fillers we find in garments are not the actual insulation. They are only a means of chopping up the air, stopping air movement and creating dead air.

Insulation for outdoor clothing has been made from many natural and man-made materials, but among the most effective insulating fillers are down, Thinsulate, Hollofil, Thermolite and Quallofil. Each of these is effective in the proper circumstances, so you must decide which is best for your hunting trips.

Down. The best-known insulating filler is not man-made. It is down, the part of the plumage on a bird that is found closest to its skin. Commercial down is a by-product of the harvesting of geese and ducks for food. Because it is a natural product that has been used effectively for many years, down is the insulator by which all others are judged.

Many people ask, "Which is best, goose or duck down?" Today, since commercially-raised geese are smaller than the commercial geese of several years ago, there is little difference except for size of down clusters in the two birds, provided they came from the same climate and had the same diet. Therefore, goose down is only slightly more efficient than duck down.

The resilience of down, or its ability to compact and come back again, is one of the most desirable traits of a down garment. The down-filled item can he compacted into a small space, smaller than a synthetic of equal warmth, and with a light shaking, will spring back.

One of the major disadvantages of down is its cost. Another disadvantage is that some hunters are allergic to down-filled equipment. They must use equipment filled with man-made fibers.

When dry, down is a champion among insulating materials. However, when it gets wet, it tends to collapse, with the possibility of leaving the wearer in a dangerous situation.

Down is good in dry cold, but not in wet cold. With this in mind, the bear hunter should not select down-filled garments or equipment for trips that will take him afield where rain, wet snow or river or lake activities are part of the trip. Down and water don't mix.

Down items can be hand washed if manufacturer's instructions are followed carefully. They can also be dry cleaned; however, if you elect to dry clean, be sure to find a professional cleaner experienced in dry-cleaning down garments.

Thermolite. Thermolite is the thin insulation of Dacron polyester used in many outer garments. A low-bulk, lightweight fiber which retains heat, Thermolite enhances the layering system's warmth and mobility.

The Dacron polyester microfiber construction of Thermolite traps air for body insulation and provides 80 percent of the insulation of high-loft fiber fillers without the bulk. Thermal tests show very positive results when compared in warmth with other thin insulations. And, critical to the system, Thermolite retains its insulation even when damp.

Thermolite is both functional and comfortable. It facilitates movement and maneuverability due to its light weight and lack of bulk. It is also non-allergenic and odorless. And, the insulation capacity of Thermolite remains intact after multiple machine washings or dry cleanings.

Hollofil. In 1973, DuPont developed a man-made fiber known as Hollofil as an insulation for outdoor garments. The Hollofil filament is short and hollow, thus giving more loft per pound than many other man-made fibers, resulting in very good insulating qualities. Another advantage to Hollofil is that, according to DuPont, it absorbs only three quarters of 1 percent moisture, so that even in the worst downpour or boat upset, it will retain its insulating value.

Since Hollofil is a short fiber, as opposed to one continuous fiber, some outdoorsmen have been concerned that the fibers would leak through the weave in the outer shell. This has not been the case with garments made by reputable manufacturers. These companies use rip-stop nylon, Cordura nylon or other high-quality outer materials which do an excellent job of holding in short or loose insulation such as Hollofil or down.

Hollofil has the added plus of being machine washable, provided the instructions are followed.

Quallofil. Another high-loft man-made insulation from Du Pont is Quallofil. Quallofil is an excellent substitute for down. Quallofil, a variation of Hollofil, was developed in 1982. It contains four holes in each fiber, which increases insulating efficiency because the holes trap more air. Quallofil is more compactable than other man-made fibers because each fiber has been coated with a slickening agent. This also makes it softer. Like the other man-made fibers, Quallofil will not absorb water and thus keeps you warm even when damp.

Unlike Hollofil, Quallofil is not loose. It is made with a backing attached and is pre-batted. The batting adds stability, so there's no shifting of the insulation during the garment's use.

Thinsulate. One of the most popular insulations in use today for hunting garments is 3M Company's "Thinsulate." As the name implies, this is a thin or low-loft insulation. According to 3M, Thinsulate provides nearly twice the warmth of down and other high-loft insulations when equal thicknesses are compared. It is breathable, allowing clothing to provide increased warmth. It retains its insulating capabilities under damp conditions. Garments insulated with Thinsulate allow improved freedom of movement because they provide warmth without bulk. Thinsulate is washable, hypo-allergenic and odorless. Because of its density, Thinsulate weighs 20 to 40 percent more than down of comparable warmth. Also, Thinsulate will not compress as well as down or Quallofil.

It is obvious that there is no single insulating material that serves all purposes. All are good when used to their best advantage. Each must be chosen with the expected use in mind.

If you think the choice of insulation is somewhat confusing, you'll be dazzled by the choice of fabrics your outer garments may be made from. There are almost as many different fabrics as there are manufacturers. You'll find that many of these are waterproof, silent in brush, tough to tear, easy to clean and long-lasting under hunting conditions.

The first rule to follow when purchasing a hunting coat, parka or jacket is to buy from a reputable dealer who handles brand-name equipment. High-quality insulated hunting garments are not cheap, but they are long-lasting and worth the cost. Your life may depend on it, and you can bet your hunting success will.

Some companies offer matching insulated trousers to go with their insulated hunting coats. These are especially useful to those who hunt bear from blinds or use boats for transportation.

The last item in this layer is by far not the least in importance—gloves. In cold climates, the bare hand holding a bow, rifle or handgun is losing heat to the cold object. If a hunter has on gloves of poor quality and the gloves are wet, he further loses heat to the cold. A good pair of gloves can prevent this heat loss and help keep the hunter warm.

Today there is no reason for a hunter to suffer from cold, wet hands. The hunting equipment industry has made great strides in

A good pair of gloves will prevent heat loss from the hand to the rifle and will keep your hands nimble for that important first shot.

handwear during the last few years, and anyone who can afford a big bear hunt can certainly afford the outstanding gloves available on the market.

The first thing that strikes the shopper looking for a new pair of gloves is the vast array of gloves now available for hunting. There are gloves for cold, wet conditions, gloves for use with horses, gloves for keeping the stand hunter's hands warm, camouflage gloves, blaze orange gloves, white gloves, mittens with a shooting finger and many more special-use gloves.

All gloves are not for all purposes. Bear hunters who hunt in wet conditions should consider insulated gloves made from Gore-Tex. Gore-Tex will keep wetness out, yet permit the perspiration of the hand to escape, thus assuring your hands of dry warmth. The drawback of many gloves made of insulation and/or Gore-Tex, as well as other materials, is that the trigger finger may be so thick that it will not fit into the trigger guard, or if it does, the fit is so tight as to inadvertently pull the trigger. All gloves should be tested for ease of trigger control *before* purchasing.

Leather gloves made from deerskin or cowhide offer the wearer a firm grip and protection from rough surfaces. These are the preferred gloves by many who hunt on horseback. Gloves made from soft cowhide or deerskin are supple and give a shooter the feel he needs when handling his firearm.

The drawbacks to leather gloves are twofold. First, they do not retain your body heat unless they are lined with some type of insulation or an insulation insert is worn under them. Secondly, leather gets wet quickly and is slow to dry. If such gloves are not dried slowly, they can become stiff.

Wool gloves were once the standby for hunters in cold weather; however, they must have a waterproof and windproof outer shell in order to keep a hunter's hands warm in cold, windy or wet conditions.

Gloves are available with nylon shells and down as insulation. These work okay when dry; once wet, down insulation is useless.

When purchasing gloves, make sure they are a good fit. They should not be so tight as to cut off circulation in the fingers or compress the insulation. Both of these conditions can cause very cold fingers. Likewise, avoid gloves that are so loose they hamper your sense of touch.

Special Protective Layers
There are times when the hats, coats, pants and boots of the outer insulated layer aren't enough. Wading creeks for brown bear or hunting mountain grizzlies in a downpour calls for a special protective layer of clothing.

The most often-used protective clothing for bear hunters is raingear, and there is perhaps no item of clothing which has improved more during the past few years. There once was a time when waterproof raingear —the kind that wouldn't leak even in a prolonged downpour—was so tight that the wearer could get just as wet on the inside from moisture released by the body. The raingear didn't breathe. This has changed, and there are several new materials on the market which can keep the wearer dry from the outside and on the inside.

Perhaps the best known of the truly waterproof fabrics is Gore-Tex. The key to the waterproof, windproof, breathable performance of Gore-Tex fabric lies in the patented microporous Gore-Tex membrane which is laminated to outer shell fabrics. The Gore-Tex membrane contains 9 billion pores per square inch, each 20,000 times smaller than a water drop, but 700 times larger than a water vapor molecule. The membrane, therefore, effectively blocks wind and weather but allows moisture from perspiration to escape.

More often than not, the grizzly hunter will find that hip boots will be a required item on his what-to-bring list. This is one more item that should be selected with extreme care. A cheap, poorly selected hip boot can almost ruin your feet within a few hours and bring your hunt to a stop.

The first step in buying hip boots is to take your time when shopping. Wear the same type clothing and socks you plan to wear when bear hunting. Try on and test walk a variety of hip boots to find which ones fit you best. I find that hip boots generally run larger in size than my leather boots. For example, I normally wear a size 12 boot, but my hip boot size is usually 11, even with heavy socks.

On the other hand, be careful not to buy them too tight. Try them out thoroughly before making a decision. Stick with well-known brand names and buy the very best you can afford. Avoid stocking-foot hip boots and get boot-foot hip boots. The boot-foot wader will give you a firmer footing, will protect your shins during inevitable stumbles over logs and stumps, and the heavier material will resist snagging. You should be careful of ankle-fit hip boots, as the big ankle boots will often wear blisters on your feet the first day out.

When buying hip boots, be sure to get the simple repair kit that comes with most. High-quality hip boots are virtually puncture-proof with normal wear, but a repair kit is a good item to have on a remote bear hunt.

The only polar bear hunts available in North America are the dog sled hunts which take place out on the ice pack of Canada's Northwest Territories. Canada North Outfitting, Inc., which runs hunts there, requires a special outer layer of clothing for each hunter in order to give him protection against the sub-zero cold. Before the hunt date, each hunter sends a tracing of his gloved hand and foot with wool stocking on, plus a good-fitting shirt and trousers. These are used as patterns by the Inuits to make caribou skin pants, parka, mitts and boots. Upon completion of the hunt, the hunter may purchase his caribou skin suit if he wishes.

After you have gone to great care and expense to purchase the right kinds of clothing for your bear hunt, there are a few simple measures you can take to help them perform at their best.

Hip boots are required equipment on almost every big bear hunt.

You should never sleep in the clothes you wear during the day. Most experienced outdoorsmen sleep in the nude. This allows their clothes to air out and keeps their clothes from absorbing moisture from the body during the night. You should also air your sleeping bag daily.

Carry along a few high-energy food bars or non-melting chocolate candy in your day pack or hunting coat pocket to nibble on during the day. Carbohydrates can provide the body with inner warmth and energy needed in cold climates.

The most important thing you can do is try to avoid sweating. Make sure your clothing is loose-fitting, and as you get warm from activity or rising temperatures, begin opening or removing layers.

Sleeping Bag And Pad

Selecting a sleeping bag and pad for bear hunting camp should be done with great care, as this is the key to a good night's sleep, which is essential to good hunting. It is an investment that should last for years.

The first thing to look for in a sleeping bag is the degree of warmth it offers. A sleeping bag keeps you warm by retaining the heat generated by your body. The holding in of this heat is made possible by the insulation with which the bag has been filled. The key element to insulation is loft, or dead air space in the insulating material. The thicker the loft, the warmer the bag.

The best-known insulating fillers used in high-quality sleeping bags are down, PolarGuard, Dacron Hollofil and Quallofil. Since grizzly hunting is often done in wet conditions, I have retired my down bag for this sport and depend upon the man-made fillers which still insulate when damp. Many hunters have replaced their down bags with Quallofil bags due to its compactibility, a real plus when packing space is limited.

The shape of your sleeping bag is something you must consider when shopping. Most sleeping bags come in one of three shapes—mummy, taper or rectangular. The mummy bag fits snugly around your body and usually has a head and neck closure for extra warmth. They usually weigh less due to their size, but offer maximum warmth. This type bag is best for backpacking or extremely cold conditions.

The taper bag does not fit as tightly around the body as does the mummy bag, but it offers more freedom of movement and packs into a small space. The rectangular bag offers the user plenty of room for stretching and turning during the night. These bags

Sleeping bags come in many shapes and weights. The conditions under which you will sleep will determine which bag is best for you. Rectangular bags (top left and bottom left) provide more room for movement while sleeping. But for the extra weight, these bags seldom hold your body's heat as well as a tight-fitting mummy bag.

usually don't have a hood. Also, they weigh more than the mummy or taper bag and take up more packing space. You might choose a rectangular bag when space and weight are not considerations. They are very comfortable bags to use in a base camp.

Since sleeping bag construction varies greatly among manufacturers, rule number one for buying sleeping bags is to buy from a reputable dealer who handles brand-name equipment. Bargain hunting can be a mistake.

Rule number two is to decide how much insulation you need for your bear camp. This varies from person to person. If your camping is mostly done during cool to cold months as most bear hunts are, you need a bag that will allow you to sleep comfortably at low temperatures. The best solution is to rent a quality sleeping bag and use it on a cold weather camping trip. Then adjust up or down in insulation.

Rule number three is don't let someone talk you into a backpack bag or mummy bag unless you need lightweight camping gear. I find that I sleep much more comfortably in a full-size sleeping bag that has a zipper across the lower end and up one side. On warm nights, I leave the bag unzipped and pull the top over me as the night cools. The full-size bag also gives me more room for moving my legs.

Once you get a good sleeping bag, take care of it. Make it a daily practice to air it when in camp. This airing will help eliminate moisture build-up, a common occurrence on many camping trips, as well as restoring loft to the insulation.

You will want to go one step further to assure your nights afield are restful: buy a good sleeping pad to go under the bag. While you are sleeping in your bag, the underneath portion becomes temporarily compressed, allowing body heat to escape. This heat loss can be acute if air is permitted to circulate under the bag, as when sleeping on a canvas cot. Many air mattresses and foam pads are available today, but the type that I have found to give the most dependable service is a self-inflating foam pad. Be sure to get a full-sized pad so that your entire body is comfortable. These pads are a combination of an airtight, waterproof nylon skin bonded to an open cell foam, and when inflated, air is trapped within the foam pad. When you lie on the pad, your weight pressurizes the trapped air. The pressurized air supports you off the ground and minimizes foam compression under your hips and shoulders. It can make a cold spike camp feel like a Hilton.

A binocular is essential on a big bear hunt.

The pressurized air also maximizes foam loft for greatest insulation. Unlike air mattresses, which have no insulation, these pads have four times the insulation of the closed-cell foam pads used by many backpackers.

If you are accustomed to sleeping on a pillow, take an inflatable or compressible foam pillow on your bear hunt with you. I have seen many otherwise properly-equipped hunters sleep poorly from not having a comfortable pillow. Sound, restful sleep is important on a bear hunt.

Miscellaneous

Long hours spent glassing valleys, mountain slopes and beaches are a major part of the bear hunt, and one of the most-used items on these hunts is a good binocular. This is not the piece of equipment to try to save a few dollars on, as cheap optics can make a day of glassing miserable, with the evening spent nursing a headache.

Since most bear hunts involve a lot of walking and sometimes climbing over rocks or through timber, a medium-sized binocular is usually the best choice. Compact binoculars have a small objective lens, making their use limited in low light conditions. In addition, prolonged use can cause eye strain.

The large objective lens binoculars, while having good light-gathering capability, are large in body size and often heavy. Thus the reason for the mid-size binoculars, such as the 7X30 or

9X35. They have good light-gathering capability and are usually lightweight, weighing around 1¼ pounds.

Other features on binoculars are very much a personal choice. For bear hunting, the magnification should be from seven to nine power. Whether your binocular has center focus adjustment or individual eyepiece adjustment is up to you.

The best guide to selecting a binocular is to stay with the well-known brand names and get the best you can afford. Before making a final selection, go to your sporting goods dealer and take the time to handle a number of binoculars. Don't rush into a decision. Get a binocular that is comfortable to wear around your neck and tucked inside your jacket. Get one that you can easily adjust to your eyes and that will stay adjusted. Make sure it is clear and presents a sharp image.

The daypack you need for bear hunting is one that is larger than many of the cheaper models that are sold for carrying school books. Remember you want enough room to store shed clothing as well as carry other essential items. The day pack should be made from a strong material such as heavy cotton duck or Cordura and have padded shoulder straps for comfortable carrying. It should have one or more outside pockets that are easy to get to for such items as a canteen, binoculars, trail snack or map. This is much quicker and easier than having to dig through the main compartment where many items may be. It is also convenient to have a reinforced tie-on accessory patch. With these patches you can roll up a sweater or coat and tie it onto the outside of the pack.

Many duffel bags are available to the hunter today, but the best I have found, in size, shape and durability, is a surplus U.S. Air Force Cargo Kit Bag that measures 23 inches by 15 inches by 13 inches. I can get everything in it for a two-week grizzly hunt with the exception of my firearm and camera gear. I stress this because many hunters bring too much gear.

If your guide uses a Super Cub to get you into camp, chances are he will restrict your gear to 40 pounds, and I have hunted with outfitters who used boats who also had a 40-pound restriction.

Before you start shopping for clothing or camping gear I suggest that you talk to your guide or outfitter and get his opinion on what and how much you need. The big bear country is giant in size, and what works on Kodiak Island may not be a good idea in the Cassiar Mountains of British Columbia. Most guides and outfitters have a good idea of exactly what you need to bring with you and will send you a checklist for packing.

Your guide should give the final word on proper clothing and equipment for your hunt, as needs will vary with each area. British Columbia guide Cy Ford provides his clients with details on gear to pack.

This is especially true for polar bear hunts where much of the gear is highly specialized and may be rented or furnished by the outfitter or guide.

In closing this chapter, I encourage you to purchase your bear hunting clothing and gear early and become familiar with its use before you show up in bear camp. When I was guiding, nothing predicted the failure of a hunt quicker than a hunter arriving in camp wearing new boots and cutting tags off his gear as he unpacked. We usually wound up wasting hunting time showing him how to lay out his camp bed, put on his new underwear, try to stretch his undersize new cap and treat the blisters on his feet.

Use your equipment often enough to know how to use it properly when you reach bear camp and have your boots well broken in. Take the same pride in your personal gear as you do your rifle and load. Your hunt will go better and be a lot more fun if you do.

Being properly dressed and having the right sleeping gear for the weather conditions can be as critical to a bear hunt as having the right rifle and ammunition. It can mean the difference in success and failure, enjoyment and misery, and possibly, in life and death. It's not cheap, but neither is a big bear hunt.

6

Big Cartridges
For Big Bear

Putting a grizzly bear down for keeps is no easy task. It has been well documented since white men first encountered grizzlies that a lot of gun, combined with good marksmanship, is required, especially if the bear is excited.

One of the first big bear spotted by the Lewis and Clark Expedition was a large grizzly lying on a ridge some 300 yards from the Missouri River. Six of the expedition's best hunters slipped to within 40 yards of the bear. Four of the hunters shot their muzzleloading rifles at the bear, while two held their fire—just in case.

When the four shots were fired, two of the balls went all the way through the bear, penetrating both lungs, but the enraged bear jumped to his feet and charged the group. The two hunters who had held their fire now shot, breaking one of the bear's shoulders. Still the charge continued, straight toward the two who shot last. These two hunters dropped their rifles and raced to the river, diving off a 20-foot bluff into the water. The bear followed on their heels, splashing heavily into the brown water.

The first hunters to shoot had now reloaded, and shooting from the top of the bluff, finally put a ball through the grizzly's head. When the bear was butchered, the hunters found that eight balls had passed through its body in various directions.

Even during modern times when rifles producing fast velocities and high energy levels are used, every hunting season we hear stories of grizzlies taking a solid hit, then getting away, or worse yet, charging hunters.

In one such case, a guide had booked a pair of hunters on a combination moose and grizzly hunt. All three had rifles chambered in .300 Win. Mag. On the third morning of the hunt, the guide took the hunters to a moose carcass where a grizzly had reportedly been feeding.

When the trio got within 50 yards of the carcass, the bear, standing on a log near the bait, looked straight at them. Even with the wind in their favor, the bear had caught their scent and held his head high, trying to get a better fix on the human scent. The guide whispered to one of the hunters to get a rest and shoot. At the report of the rifle, the bear was knocked off the log and turned flips in the snow.

"Shoot again," the guide instructed the hunter. He did, but hit the bear in the left front leg. At this shot, the bear headed for the hunters.

By now, everyone was shooting. The guide put a shot into the bear's chest, and the two hunters emptied their rifles, hitting the animal at least five times in the face and throat area. Only once during those terrifying seconds did the bear lose his footing.

Still charging, the bear reached the trio. One hunter ran to the left, the other to the right, both trying to reload. The guide jumped behind a large tree, but the bear had a fix on him and was there in a second. The bear's first blow sent the guide's rifle flying and knocked the man down. Next, the bear bit the guide's left arm and then the top of his head, literally scalping him.

The two hunters had reloaded and were now trying to get a clear shot at the enraged beast. At the first opportunity, both hunters fired simultaneously from 10 feet. The bear fell on the guide. Thinking the bear dead, the hunters ran over and pulled the guide from under the animal, but as they did, the bear bawled and tried to get up. A shot to the brain finally ended the rage. The guide lived, thanks to some skillful medical attention.

This was not a large brown bear, but a mountain grizzly estimated to weigh 400 pounds. Yet he took all that the .300 Win. Mag. had to offer and put up a good fight. It takes a lot to put a grizzly down for keeps, and the hunter new to the sport needs to be keenly aware of this.

The objective in big bear hunting must always be to make a clean kill. Nothing is worse in bear hunting than not hitting a bear

It takes a lot of gun and good marksmanship to put a big bear down for keeps.

properly, either with a good shot or with the right gun and load. The mauling of the guide I described was caused when the hunter firing the first shot with his .300 Win. Mag. hit the bear too far back, missing all the vital areas. Many a good man has gone to an early grave because he—or his hunting partner—didn't hit a bear right the first time.

Selecting A Caliber/Load

Making a clean kill on a bear begins with selecting a caliber/load combination that is capable of killing a bear quickly *if* you use good marksmanship. First, however, you should know what really puts an animal down when it is struck by a bullet. During my years of guiding hunters, I found that many hunters were knowledgeable of firearms and ballistics, but few knew much about what actually killed an animal when it was hit by a fast-moving projectile.

Big game may be killed by a bullet in a number of ways. For instance, the bullet may strike the heart, cutting off the animal's blood supply. A bullet in the brain stops all vital life support

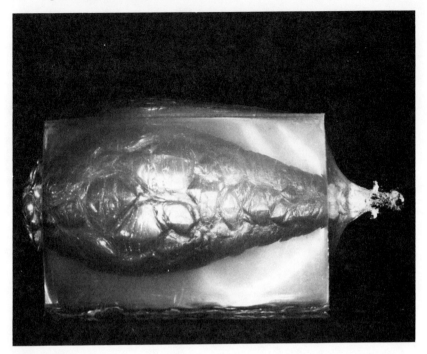

Bullet shock tests demonstrate the devastating effects of shock waves on tissues when hit by a bullet.

systems. A bullet in the lungs destroys the respiratory system. A wound to the diaphragm, a muscular membrane that aids the lungs in pumping air, can also be deadly after a period of time, as can a wound to the liver. Even a wound to a non-vital area may eventually lead to death.

With the exception of the spine or brain shot, any of these fatal hits may not knock a big bear down, allowing him to travel some distance before falling—a dangerous situation with a bear. In such cases, the hunter may blame his rifle and cartridge for not having enough "knockdown power."

However, another way a bullet can kill a bear and take him off his feet instantly is with shock, more precisely "hydrostatic shock."

Shock waves are carried very rapidly at full force by water, which an animal's body is primarily composed of, and break down the solid materials—in this case, the bear's vitals—within the water. It is this shock, caused by the transfer of energy from the bullet into the tissue of the animal, and not the bullet itself, that we know as "knockdown power."

When selecting a caliber and load, hunters are too often concerned with only the trajectory of their bullet at longer ranges, failing to consider the loss of energy by the bullet and the importance of retaining enough downrange energy to put a big bear down. Anyone hunting big bear should select a caliber/load combination that delivers enough downrange kinetic energy, or "knockdown power," for the extreme range at which a shot may be taken. Ample kinetic energy will break heavy bones, make a sizable wound channel, destroy vital organs and produce immobilizing shock.

Please take note that this is *downrange* energy and not muzzle energy. The difference is great, and too many hunters are only aware of their load's muzzle energy, not the energy level where the animal is.

Caliber Selection

It is necessary in caliber selection to choose a caliber with enough powder capacity in the case to push the properly constructed bullet fast enough to get the downrange energy level needed to put a bear down.

While there are no hard and fast rules on how much downrange energy is enough for a bear, it is generally accepted that 2,000 foot-pounds is sufficient for bear weighing up to 600 pounds, and 2,800 foot-pounds of energy is needed for bear of over 600 pounds. This rules out a lot of rifle calibers fast. Yes, I know big bear have been taken with such small calibers as .17 Rem., .22 Hornet, .222 Rem., .223 Rem. and .30-30 Win., but these were exceptions. Who knows how many bear have been injured by puny calibers and how many hunters mauled as a result of such a poor choice?

Calibers and bullet weights that maintain 2,000 foot-pounds of energy with factory loads out to 150 yards, the maximum range for shooting big bear, according to almost every grizzly outfitter I've talked to, include:

.270 Win. (130-grain bullet)
.270 Wthby Mag. (130- and 150-grain bullets)
.280 Rem. (150- and 165-grain bullets)
.284 Win. (150-grain bullet)
7mm Rem. Mag. (125-, 150- and 175-grain bullets)
7mm Wthby Mag. (139-, 154- and 175-grain bullets)

Cartridges the author feels are suitable for big bear (l to r): .300 Win. Mag., .300 Wthby Mag., .308 Norma Mag., 8mm Rem., .338 Win. Mag., .340 Wthby Mag., .375 H&H Mag., .378 Wthby Mag., .458 Win. Mag. and .460 Wthby Mag.

.30-06 (150-, 165- and 180-grain bullets)
.300 Win. Mag. (150-, 180- and 220-grain bullets)
.300 H&H Mag. (150-, 180- and 220-grain bullets)
.300 Wthby Mag. (150- and 180-grain bullets)
.308 Win. (180-grain bullet)
8mm Rem. Mag. (185- and 220-grain bullets)
.338 Win. Mag. (200-, 225- and 250-grain bullets)
.340 Wthby Mag. (200- and 250-grain bullets)
.350 Rem. Mag. (200-grain bullet)
.375 H&H Mag. (270- and 300-grain bullets)
.378 Wthby Mag. (300-grain bullet)
.458 Win. Mag. (500-grain bullet)
.460 Wthby Mag. (500-grain bullet).

Popular rifle calibers and bullet weights that have a retained energy level of 2,800 foot-pounds at 150 yards are:
.300 Win. Mag. (180-grain bullet)
.308 Norma Mag. (180-grain bullet)
.300 Wthby Mag. (150- and 180-grain bullets)
.338 Win. Mag. (200-, 225-, and 250-grain bullets)
.340 Wthby Mag. (200- and 250-grain bullets)
.375 H&H Mag. (270-grain bullet)
.378 Wthby Mag. (300-grain bullet)
.458 Win. Mag. (500-grain bullet)
.460 Wthby Mag. (500-grain bullet).

Comparative Rifle Ballistics					
Caliber	**Bullet Wt. (Grs.)**	**Muzzle Velocity (FPS)**	**Muzzle Energy (Ft-Lbs)**	**Downrange Energy (Ft-Lbs)**	
				100 Yds.	**200 Yds.**
.338 Win. Mag.	200	2,960	3,892	3,138	2,506
.30-30 Win.	170	2,200	1,827	1,356	990
.35 Rem.	200	2,080	1,922	1,281	841

An illustration of why some "old favorite" deer rifles don't measure up to big bear. It takes approximately 2,000 foot-pounds of energy to down a bear weighing up to 600 pounds, and approximately 2,800 foot-pounds of energy to down a bear weighing more than 600 pounds.

Factory Load Ballistics For Big Bear Rifle Calibers					
Caliber	**Bullet Wt. (Grs.)**	**Muzzle Velocity (FPS)**	**Muzzle Energy (Ft-Lbs)**	**Downrange Energy (Ft-Lbs)**	
				100 Yds.	**200 Yds.**
.300 Wthby Mag.	180	3,300	4,300	3,753	3,226
	220	2,905	4,000	3,050	2,206
.300 H&H Mag.	180	2,880	3,315	2,785	2,325
.300 Win. Mag.	180	2,960	3,503	3,012	2,579
	220	2,680	3,510	2,928	2,426
.308 Norma Mag.	180	3,020	3,646	3,168	2,740
8mm Rem. Mag.	185	3,080	3,898	3,132	2,495
	220	2,830	3,913	3,255	2,689
.338 Win. Mag.	200	2,960	3,892	3,138	2,506
	225	2,780	3,862	3,306	2,816
.340 Wthby Mag.	200	3,210	4,577	3,857	3,228
	210	3,180	4,717	3,996	3,365
	250	2,850	4,510	3,515	2,710
.375 H&H Mag.	270	2,690	4,339	3,512	2,813
	300	2,530	4,265	3,427	2,724
.378 Wthby Mag.	270	3,180	6,064	4,688	3,570
	300	2,925	5,700	4,380	3,325
.458 Win. Mag.	510	2,040	4,714	3,549	2,641
.460 Wthby Mag.	500	2,700	8,095	6,370	4,968

The .30-30 Win. (left) and .35 Rem. (center), often mistaken as big bear cartridges, seem puny beside the .378 Wthby Mag.

Ask inexperienced bear hunters to name the best calibers for hunting big bear and you will hear arguments for everything from the .30-30 Win. on up. Ask the same question of those hunters who have faced big bear, and the minimum caliber usually starts with the .300 Win. Mag.

To hear the opinions of those who face grizzlies regularly, I surveyed many of the professional grizzly guides in Alaska, the Yukon and British Columbia, asking what rifle caliber they preferred that their hunters use. The .338 Win. Mag. was by far the favorite by both inland and brown bear guides.

A few inland grizzly guides, like Ken Kyllo of Hudson's Hope, British Columbia, said they would take a hunter using a .30-06 with an appropriate load, provided the hunter is very familiar and proficient with his rifle and load. Otherwise, he wants his hunters to use a .300 Win. Mag. or larger caliber.

Larry Rivers, master guide from Talkeetna, Alaska, wants his hunters to use at least a .300 Win. Mag. on inland grizzlies and

.338 Win. Mag. or .375 H&H Mag. on brown bear. Cy Ford, who guides along the coast of British Columbia, is very specific. He wants his hunters to use a .338 Win. Mag. with a 250-grain Nosler Partition bullet.

The bottom line in caliber selection for a big bear hunt is to first get your guide's recommendation. He is experienced at bear hunting in the area you will be in and will have a definite idea of what you should use. Use a caliber and hunting load that you have practiced with and can hit your target with from 150 yards. I would much rather take a 75-yard shot at a brown bear using a .338 Win. Mag. that I was comfortable shooting and had confidence in than to have a powerful .458 Win. Mag. of which I was scared. As we will discuss in Chapter 9, poor bullet placement can be a deadly mistake when hunting big bear.

Based on my guide survey, the .30-06 is generally considered too small and the .458 Win. Mag. too large. All calibers in between these two are considered by most to be much more effective, with the .338 Win. Mag. the top choice, especially if other game, such as caribou or moose, are to be hunted at the same time.

Bullet Construction

Almost all of the guides I talked to wanted their hunters to use bullets that weighed 200 grains or more and were constructed to hold together for deep penetration and controlled expansion.

For the kinetic energy to be transferred from the bullet entering the animal's body into the shock waves which destroy the animal's nervous system, the bullet must be constructed to expand in a controlled fashion as it travels into the animal.

It is this mushrooming, or bulldozer effect, of the expanding bullet which transfers the energy and causes the deadly hydrostatic shock.

A thin-jacketed bullet will break up on impact with a grizzly's shoulder, while a steel-jacketed bullet may pass completely through the bear's body, transferring little energy, causing little hydrostatic shock and thus not putting the animal down. Instead, controlled expansion and penetration, with retention of much of the original weight, are the necessary features for a big bear bullet.

In order to achieve this, the bullet must he constructed so that the core will stay in the jacket to guarantee the retained weight necessary for adequate penetration. This is done by locking the core to the jacket. A Bitterroot bullet, the choice of many bear

Controlled expansion of a bullet is essential for big bear hunting. The .338 Win. Mag. gives controlled expansion and penetration, while retaining much of its original weight.

hunters, gives this desired result by having a heavy copper-tubing jacket bonded to the lead core so they will not separate.

The Nosler Partition, perhaps the most popular bullet in use by bear hunters today, locks the core to the jacket to assure mass retention by using a partition in the jacket. The forward core expands, while the rear core stays intact. Remington makes its famous CoreLokt bullets perform properly by using a heavy midsection jacket to lock the metal jacket and lead cone together.

The selection of high-quality factory loads in the big-bear calibers is constantly growing. Such ammunition manufacturers as Remington, Winchester, Federal, Norma, Weatherby and Hornady offer enough choices that the most discriminating hunter can find a factory load that will shoot well in his rifle.

Many hunters now handload ammunition, and by testing a wide variety of loads in their rifle, they can usually obtain better results than with factory loads. However, guides offer a word of caution in regard to handloading ammunition for bear hunting: More misfires occur on hunts when handloads are used.

The handloading hunter should consider that one primer with a small amount of case lube on it may cost him the trophy of a lifetime. Or, the guide may have to finish off a bear in case a second or third shot is necessary and the hunter's rifle won't fire. I have personally seen the look on a hunter's face when his handloads wouldn't fire at a trophy grizzly slowly walking across a clearing 75 yards away. It can make the trip off a mountain long and silent.

7

Big Rifles
For Big Bear

Rifle selection is a personal matter, with most hunters having some very definite opinions on which is the best rifle for a particular species of big game. The same is true with bear rifles, except some thought must be given to the fact that a bear can be a dangerous critter, and a second, third and fourth shot may be necessary to get the job done properly.

Some bear hunters want the firepower of a semi-automatic rifle, while others want the challenge and accuracy of a single-shot rifle. A few even choose the double rifle.

However, most hunters and virtually every bear guide I have discussed rifles with prefers a good bolt-action rifle. They are quick and simple to use, accurate, and can take the abusive weather and other conditions that come with hunting big bear. While they don't have the rapid firepower of the semi-automatic, they do offer a third or fourth shot, and in some cases, a fifth, should such be required.

Bolt-Action

Browning A-Bolt. This rifle is available in these big bear calibers: .375 H&H Mag., .338 Win. Mag. and .300 Win. Mag. This 7¼-pound rifle has a thin-bodied bolt with three locking lugs and a short, 60-degree bolt throw. It has a plunger-type ejector, recessed boltface and fluted bolt surface. The 26-inch barrel is

Two Sako rifles: the Lightweight Hunter (top) and the Lightweight Deluxe.

free-floating and glass-bedded at the recoil lug. It has a top tang, a thumb-operated safety and a hinged floorplate with detachable box magazine. The stock on all three big-bear calibers is a wooden continental style with cheekpiece; however, those who like a synthetic stock can get a graphite-fiberglass composite stock on the .338 Win. Mag. and .300 Win. Mag. All stocks come with a recoil pad.

Parker-Hale M81 Classic, 1200M Super, 1200CM Super, 1100M African Magnum. Weights of these rifles are 7¾ pounds, 7½ pounds, 7½ pounds and 9½ pounds, respectively.

They are available in .300 Win. Mag. (M81 Classic, 1200M Super, 1200CM Super); .375 H&H Mag. (1100M African Magnum); and .458 Win. Mag. (1100M African Magnum).

These rifles feature a glass-bedded wood stock with recoil pad, hinged floorplate and the strong Mauser bolt action. A set trigger is offered as an option. All models have a 24-inch barrel. The M81 Classic and 1100M African Magnum have a four-round magazine capacity, and the 1200s have a three-round capacity.

Remington 700. This model is offered in .300 Win. Mag. (7¾ pounds), .338 Win. Mag. (7¾ pounds), 8mm Rem. Mag. (10 pounds), .375 H&H Mag. (9 pounds) and .458 Win. Mag. (9 pounds). The Model 700 action features solid steel lockup in a receiver milled from ordnance-grade steel. It has a wooden stock and hinged floorplate.

The hammer-forged barrel is 24 inches long, and the magazine capacity is three. The 8mm Rem. Mag., .375 H&H Mag. and .458

The Weatherby Mark V Euromark Model rifle, equipped with a 3-9X44 Supreme scope on a Buehler mount.

Win. Mag. are available only from Remington's custom shop. Remington's custom shop now also offers the new .416 Remington—another great big bear round.

Ruger M-77. Available to the big-bear hunter in .300 Win. Mag. (7 pounds), .338 Win. Mag. (7 pounds) and .458 Win. Mag. (8¾ pounds), the M-77 bolt-action rifle is noted for strength. The barrel, receiver, bolt and other metal parts are made from heat-treated chrome molybdenum steel. It has two massive front locking lugs and a positive long extractor. The safety, which is mounted in the heavy metal of the tang, is of the shotgun type and easy to use. It has a hinged floorplate and wooden stock with recoil pad. Exclusive to Ruger are integral scope bases incorporated into the receiver. The barrel length is 24 inches.

Sako. Sako rifles come in many variations, with calibers available to the big-bear hunter in .300 Win. Mag., .300 Wthby Mag., .338 Win. Mag. and .375 H&H Mag. Weights vary from 7 to 8¼ pounds, depending upon stock and barrel length. The Sako action features a one-piece forged bolt and bolt handle, chrome molybdenum steel forged receiver, twin lug, front locking lug system, integral scope mount rails, three-way adjustable trigger and a hinged floorplate. A number of options are available. Barrel length may vary from the short 18½-inch carbine length—great for hunting bear in thick brush—to 24 inches. Stock variations range from Mannlicher-style to fiberglass.

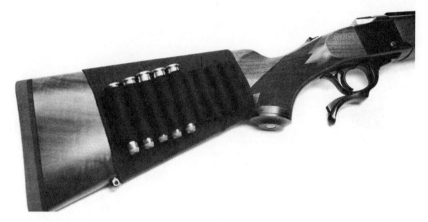

When hunting big bear, a butt stock shell holder, like this one from Michaels of Oregon, is a necessity for single shot rifles and an insurance policy when using a bolt action.

Steyr-Mannlicher Model S. Weighing 8½ pounds, the Model S is available for big-bear hunters in .300 Win. Mag., .375 H&H Mag. and .458 Win. Mag. It has a hammer-forged barrel, adjustable trigger, detachable rotary four-round magazine and a boltface which surrounds the cartridge case head when chambered for maximum strength and minimum play. The wood stock has an oil finish and recoil pad. Two barrel lengths are available—25.6 inches and a 20-inch shortened version that works well in heavy cover.

Weatherby Mark V. The weight of this rifle varies from 7¼ pounds to 10½ pounds in .300 Wthby Mag., .340 Wthby Mag., and .378 Wthby Mag. Its action features nine locking lugs, enclosed bolt sleeve and cartridge case head completely enclosed in the bolt and barrel. The hammer-forged barrel comes in 24- and 26-inch lengths, depending on the caliber. A wood stock is standard, but fiberglass is available on some models.

Winchester Model 70. At a weight of 7¾ pounds, the Model 70 comes in .300 Win. Mag., .300 Wthby Mag., .338 Win. Mag., .375 H&H Mag. and .458 Win. Mag. Receiver and integral lugs are machined from chrome molybdenum steel; the bolt body and locking lugs are machined from ordnance steel. It has a Winchester three-position safety and adjustable trigger. The barrel is 24 inches long on all models except the .458 Win. Mag., which is 22 inches.

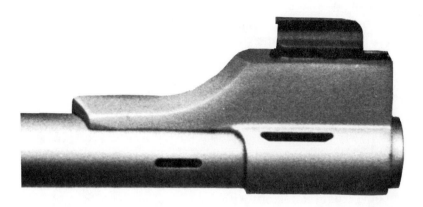

A Mag-na-ported barrel is a welcome option on larger caliber big bear guns. It can reduce felt recoil and muzzle jump.

All models come with a wood stock, with McMillan's fiberglass "Winlite" stock available on some models.

Semi-Automatic

Browning BAR. The semi-automatic rifle of choice is the Browning BAR. It weighs 8⅜ pounds and is available in .300 Win. Mag. and .338 Win. Mag. It has a gas-operated action, featuring a seven-lug rotary bolt. Its box-type, removable magazine holds three cartridges. It has a wood stock with recoil pad.

Single-Shot

Ruger No. 1. The most popular single-shot rifle is the Ruger No. 1, which weighs 8 pounds and is available in .300 Win. Mag., .300 Wthby Mag., .338 Win. Mag., .375 H&H Mag. and .458 Win. Mag. All calibers have a 26-inch barrel, except the last two which have a 24-inch barrel. Hunters who choose a single-shot rifle for big-bear hunting are advised to carry extra cartridges on a Michaels of Oregon Rifle Butt Stock Shell Holder to speed up reloading.

A growing number of rifles are now being offered with a synthetic or weather-proof laminated stock. Since much of the big bear habitat is a wet environment, serious consideration should be given to buying a rifle with one of these stocks or replacing the wood stock with one of the many drop-in synthetic or laminated stocks available today. A standard wood stock subjected day after day to driving rain, wet bushes, creek crossings and the like may swell, affecting the accuracy of the firearm.

Rifle Options And Accessories

Many hunters dislike the recoil and muzzle jump associated with heavy calibers used on big bear. If this is causing you to have poor marksmanship, I suggest you spend the extra money to get your rifle barrel modified by Mag-na-port or KDF Recoil Arrestor. Either of these processes can reduce felt recoil and muzzle jump, thereby helping you concentrate on good marksmanship practices.

When you are preparing for your hunt, keep in mind that some rifles come from the factory with poor accuracy built in, and most will shoot one load more accurately than others. In fact, your rifle may not shoot some loads accurately enough for hunting dangerous game. There is only one way to check this out in your bear rifle: spend several days on the range shooting the rifle from a benchrest with a variety of bear hunting loads until you are satisfied that you have an accurate rifle matched to a good hunting load. For my own bear hunting, I want a heavy caliber rifle that is capable of shooting a two-inch five-shot group at 150 yards with my hunting load.

At the time you are doing this range work, you should be shooting the same scope on your rifle that you intend to use on your bear hunt. Riflescopes and mounting systems take a pounding on these big rifles shooting powerful loads, and occasionally they will shoot loose or a reticle will move. Get the best riflescope and mounting system you can find, and watch it carefully as you do your range work.

The selection of a riflescope for bear hunting is easy if that is the only species of game to be hunted. Most guides agree that the best range is within 100 yards to give the shooter the best target possible for proper bullet placement and to have as much energy as possible remaining in the bullet. Most guides don't want a shot over 150 yards, and shots over 100 yards are usually reserved only for proven marksmen at a good target. For safety reasons, some guides avoid stalks putting the hunter at ranges under 50 yards. Not many bear go down in their tracks with one shot.

Considering the short ranges within which bear are likely to be shot, most hunters prefer a 1X or 1.5X scope for hunting brown bear in the thick cover found along the coast. If longer shots are anticipated, a 1.5-5X, such as the Leupold Vari-X III, is great. It can be turned down in thick cover and moved up for bear feeding

The prospective big bear hunter should spend many days on the rifle range, testing the rifle and loads before embarking on the hunt.

on open slides or tidal flats. If other game, such as moose or caribou, is to be hunted with the rifle, a higher-powered variable scope may be chosen. However, the variable should include a power at least as low as 2X for the really close shots.

As with all your equipment, your choice of riflescope should be the best you can afford. Wet conditions, heavy recoil, bumps and knocks day after day in boats or on stalks will take a heavy toll on cheap scopes. It is sad to see a once-in-a-lifetime hunt ruined by a fogged scope or one that won't hold a zero. This is not the place to cut corners to pay the plane fare.

Since bear hunting can mean hours of walking, often up steep slopes, across swollen creeks, on snow slides and many times on snowshoes, a sling is an important addition to a rifle. Every bear hunter should also know how to shoot using a sling position, both sitting and kneeling. Bear hunting is not the place for unaided, off-hand shooting. A sling can give you the edge if no other rest is available.

Also be sure to carry a compact rifle cleaning kit with you. A rifle takes a lot of abuse on a bear hunt, and a nightly cleaning is not a bad idea.

Another shooting accessory the bear hunter should have is a strong, lockable, hard-bodied gun case to pack your rifle in while flying commercially. From that point on, you will want a well-padded soft case to protect your rifle when in bush planes or in boats.

Finally, if you are going on a horseback hunt, check with your guide in advance to see if you or he furnishes a saddle scabbard. If it's up to you, consider the Cordura scabbards from Michaels of Oregon. I have found them to do a better job of protecting my rifle than traditional leather scabbards.

8

Hunting Big Bear
With A Handgun,
Bow or Muzzleloader

Hunting big bear with a modern rifle is a challenge, as there is some risk involved. Even with multiple shot capability, the first shot is what it's all about. However, some hunters want an even greater challenge and choose to hunt big bear with either a handgun, bow or muzzleloading rifle.

Any of these three means of taking a bear requires that the hunter get as close to his game as possible. Most of the handguns suitable for taking big bear are single-shot, meaning a good first shot to break down the bear is a must, as the second shot is slow in coming. Bowhunters know that an arrow kills a bear by causing hemorrhaging and that the bear will stay on his feet for at least a few critical seconds, plenty of time for a charge, even after taking a hit in the vitals. The muzzleloading rifle hunter usually has single-shot capacity, unless a double rifle is used. And, due to the cloud of white smoke it produces when fired, the muzzleloading rifle identifies the position of the shooter for the bear instantly. In short, any one of these three methods of bear hunting can be one of the greatest challenges in the hunting world.

Who should attempt a challenge of such magnitude? Obviously, the first answer to this question is one who has mastered the skill of shooting the handgun, bow or muzzleloading rifle. Each of the three requires hours and hours of practice to master the marksmanship necessary to make the first shot count, even when hands are wet and cold, knees are shaking from excitement and the body is heaving from an exhausting stalk.

Next, the hunter must have the ability to pinpoint the exact spot on the bear he wants to hit. A big bear at 15 yards is a massive target, but little of that mass is the target you want to hit. It requires some study and a lot of concentration and self-control when the moment of truth arrives.

The third part of the answer to this question was given to me by my friend Bob Good, a nationally-known handgun hunter who has taken brown bear with a single-shot handgun. Good acknowledges that grizzlies and brown bear have been successfully taken by handgun hunters, and will continue to be, but cautions that a hunt for either of these should be conducted with extreme caution and care. ''The hunter should always be backed up by an experienced, competent guide armed with a heavy caliber rifle,'' Good advises. ''The guide should understand that getting a bear with a handgun is important to you, and that once he fires and hits the bear, it cannot be classified as a handgun kill (for trophy records). He must be experienced enough on bear to rapidly judge if your hits are going to be quickly fatal to the bear, or if you may be put in a life-threatening situation. And you must have the trust and confidence in your backup, so that if he fires, you don't come all unglued because he felt he had to fire to protect your collective posteriors from a potential chewing. Remember that the personal safety of the guide and hunter must be paramount at all times. If there is the slightest question, the guide should shoot instantly, and since it will always be a judgment call, you must be willing to abide by the call. If you are not willing to accept those conditions, then don't hunt the big bear, or any other dangerous game for that matter.''

This advice applies equally to bowhunters and muzzleloading rifle hunters. Since there are relatively few of us who can legally hunt the big bear without a guide, having a qualified backup is usually automatic.

I admire those who hunt the big bear by these challenging means, and it is one of my greatest hunting goals to take a big bear with each of these methods.

Handgunning For Bear

Mention hunting big bear with a handgun, and someone will quickly start talking about the .44 Magnum and all its power. The fact of the matter is that the .44 Mag. is not the most powerful

Hours of practice, both at the bench and under field conditions, are essential before attempting to hunt bear with a handgun.

handgun caliber in the world, as movies and TV would have us believe, and it is not a good choice for big bear. Granted, some big bear have been taken with a .44 Mag., but even most of those hunters will admit that it is marginal on a bear that is totally calm when shot and less effective on an excited bear.

Larry Kelly, one of America's best-known handgun hunters, has shot brown bear in both situations and can testify to the limits of the .44 Mag. Kelly took a large brown bear, which now ranks twenty-sixth in the Safari Club International record book, with one shot from a .44 Mag. 8⅜-inch barreled Ruger Stalker with Federal 240-grain JTC-SIL ammo. He fired at approximately 50 yards after a very long stalk.

Kelly was shooting down on the bear, and the bullet went in behind the shoulder and into the heart. The bear began to snap at the entrance hole in its shoulder, collapsed and rolled down the hill. It never knew anyone was around.

When Kelly approached the fallen bear, he still fired a second shot into the animal just to be on the safe side. However, not long

Larry Kelly with a large brown bear he took with a .44 Magnum handgun.

after that, Kelly and his guide were charged by a much smaller bear, and six shots from his .44 Magnum into the bear's chest had little stopping effect. Kelly told me the bear seemed more concerned with the muzzle blast than taking the 240-grain bullets into his vitals. The guide finished off the bear with his .375 H&H Mag. rifle.

While I was working on this chapter, I got a call from a hunter headed to Alaska for a moose and caribou hunt. He was naturally excited about his hunt, and he told me all about the .44 Mag. he would carry on his hunt as protection from bear. I've heard this story dozens of times. According to all the information I can gather, *there is no documented case of a hunter ever having saved himself from a bear attack by pulling out his trusty .44 Mag. and dropping the enraged animal.* As Kelly found out, even at point-blank range, if you don't put a bullet into the brain, you've got big trouble.

For those who insist on hunting big bear with the .44 Mag. handgun, Larry Kelly suggests that you use hot handloads with the 305-grain Cor-Bon bullet or 320-grain SSK bullet. These two are what he uses for all large game, including elephants.

There are a number of handgun choices in .44 Mag. that are suitable for hunting. Ruger offers the Super Redhawk and Super Blackhawk. The double-action Super Redhawk is designed for hunting with an integral scope mounting system. While the Super Blackhawk is a well-known single-action .44 Magnum, one custom version of this gun that has been outfitted for the big game hunter is available from Magnum Sales Limited. Called "The Stalker," it features a 2X Leupold pistol scope mounted with the strong SSK Industries mounting system and sling swivels with sling. The barrel has been Mag-na-ported. Magnum Sales Limited has also outfitted the Smith & Wesson Model 629 in a similar fashion, plus reworked the action. This double-action outfit is named the "Smith & Wesson Stalker."

The revolver that is probably getting the most attention from big bear handgun hunters is the .454 Casull made by Freedom Arms. It comes in barrel lengths from 4¾ to 7½ inches, with most big bear hunters choosing the longer. This is an extremely strong five-shot, single-action revolver chambered in .454 Casull that can generate over a ton of energy at the muzzle, nearly twice that of a .44 Mag. In fact, the .454 Casull 300-grain factory load delivers more energy at 200 yards than the .44 Magnum, 240-grain factory load has at the muzzle.

I think we will see a number of record book grizzlies and brown bear being taken with this pistol in the near future, as it is finding favor with a growing number of hunters. If a bear hunter feels compelled to carry a backup sidearm, I would heartily recommend the .454 Casull in the 4¾-inch barrel length.

The most popular caliber for big bear among handgun hunters is the .375 JDJ, and with good reason. Numerous big bear shot with this caliber have gone down without any trouble. The .375 JDJ is a wildcat caliber developed by firearms expert J.D. Jones. It is a .444 Marlin case necked down to accept the .375 bullet. It has prairie-dog accuracy out to distances much farther than anyone should be shooting at a bear and enough energy to kill an elephant.

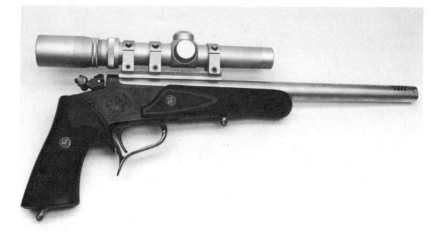

The .375 JDJ barrel on a Thompson/Center Contender frame.

The firearm this outstanding cartridge is shot from is a Thompson/Center Contender outfitted with an SSK Industries .375 JDJ Barrel. While I had long been a Contender fan, my introduction to this caliber was on a mixed-bag hunt a few years ago in the Brooks Range. I was hunting with Lucky Nightingale, a world-class handgun hunter. On that hunt, Lucky took a moose, caribou, Dall ram and grizzly with a .375 JDJ Contender. It made a believer out of me.

While hunting with the .375 JDJ the following year, he took a brown bear on the Alaskan Peninsula at 80 yards, using a load consisting of 48 grains of IMR 4895 under a 270-grain Hornady spirepoint bullet. The first shot hit the lungs. The bear started to run, and Lucky rapidly reloaded the Contender single-shot and put the second round through the bear's hump. He dropped. The bear's hide squared 10 feet 1 inch, and it had a 28-inch skull.

I consider the .375 JDJ caliber in the T/C Contender to be one of the all-time best handgun hunting combinations. When used with the SSK T'SOB mounting system and a good pistol scope, 1.5-inch groups at 100 yards can be expected from hunting loads.

Since the Contender is a single-shot pistol, anyone considering hunting dangerous game such as bear should wear a Michaels of Oregon Wrist Band Cartridge Holder on his wrist to make reloading faster. It holds six cartridges in a fast and easy to get to position. Michaels of Oregon also offers a sturdy nylon shoulder holster for the scoped T/C Contender, which is a convenient way to

The author predicts that the Freedom Arms .454 Casull, which is finding favor with a growing number of big bear hunters, will take a number of record book grizzlies and brown bear.

carry the handgun when hunting in grizzly country. It leaves the hands free for moving limbs or climbing.

The hunter who convinced me to hunt with the .375 JDJ was Bob Good, whom I mentioned earlier. Bob, while hunting deer at my hunting lodge, encouraged me to take his .375 JDJ Contender out to the rifle range and give it a try. It was love at first shot. The big handgun had manageable recoil and was extremely accurate. I wondered how it would perform on big bear. The answer was quick in coming.

Soon after our hunt, I got a letter from Bob telling me about a brown bear he had taken with the .375 JDJ using 280-grain Hornady roundnose bullets. He shot at a range of 60 yards, twice the distance he wanted but as close as he could get to the bear. The bullet entered at and broke the last two ribs, passed through the lower left and upper right lungs, then passed through the neck, where it severed both the carotid artery and jugular vein. The bullet stopped just under the skin of the neck in a reverse position, with the base protruding from the neck muscle. The jacket was still attached and had opened with the nose to about .55 inch, giving the impression of an upside-down umbrella.

The bullet had penetrated approximately three feet. At the shot, the bear jumped out of sight, but from his position and the condition of the grass around him, Good concluded that he had died in mid-air on the jump, hit the bank dead, and rolled over

For a fast second shot when using the single-shot pistol, a wrist band cartridge holder is recommended.

backwards. He was on his back with all four feet in the air. The big brown bear still had a salmon clutched in his teeth.

Since then, I have been hunting a variety of game with the .375 JDJ and find it to be all I was told.

Another good caliber for handgun hunting big bear is the .45-70, which is also available in an SSK barrel to drop into the T/C Contender frame. It is accurate, and as J.D. Jones puts it, "...the best 150-yard sledgehammer for hunting available in the Contender," which puts it well within grizzly range. Some good factory loads are available for this caliber, and handloads with the Speer 400-grain bullet do a good job, expanding to about .85 inch. Cast bullets also work well in .45-70 loads.

Pistol scopes and mounting systems for any of these big-bore handguns should be chosen with care. Due to the recoil, you should get the strongest system you can find. I have used the SSK T'SOB and Weaver mounting systems without any problems. Burris, Leupold and Bausch & Lomb pistol scopes are also favorites among many bear hunters using handguns.

When choosing a pistol scope, consider one with a 1.5X to 5X magnification. Chances are, you will use the 1.5X to 3X most of the time, but it's nice to have the extra capability.

If you want to hunt big bear with a handgun, go to Alaska. Non-residents cannot take a handgun into Canada, and handgun ownership of residents is very limited. If you are a Canadian,

Bob Good with a brown bear he took using a .375 JDJ.

Pistol cartridges commonly used on big bear include (l to r): .44 Magnum, .454 Casull, .375 JDJ and the .45-70.

check with your local laws to see if you can hunt big bear with a handgun there.

I heard about a hunter who was going to the Yukon for a spring grizzly hunt. At the last moment, he decided to leave his rifle at home and take his hunting handgun. His hunt was abruptly stopped at the border. So if you want to hunt with your handgun, think Alaska.

Factory Load Ballistics For Big Bear Handgun Calibers					
Caliber	**Bullet Wt. (Grs.)**	**Muzzle Velocity (FPS)**	**Muzzle Energy (Ft-Lbs)**	**Downrange Energy (Ft-Lbs)**	
				50 Yds.	**100 Yds.**
.44 Rem. Mag.	240	1,180	741	623	543
.454 Casull	240	1,875	1,873	1,494	1,186
	260	1,800	1,870	1,516	1,225
	300	1,600	1,705	1,417	1,181
.375 JDJ	270	1,990	2,373	2,198	2,043
.45-70	400	1,631	2,365	2,150	1,995

Bowhunting For Bear

I had the good fortune of hunting with Fred Bear for several hunting seasons, and it was always the highlight of the hunt to hear Fred tell about his big bear hunts. During his long hunting career, he took polar, brown and grizzly bear with a bow.

Fred Bear was one of the world's top bear hunters with a bow.

The last time Fred and I hunted together, he told me that his greatest hunt ever was a brown bear hunt he took during the early 1960s. Fred, his guide and a photographer were checking out a beach area from a small boat. When they rounded a small point, they saw a big brown walking out of the alders onto the beach about a half-mile away. The hunters shut off the boat motor and slowly, quietly made their way to the beach, while the bear proceeded to feed on something in the sand. At one point, the bear waded into the water and lay on his back with only his head and feet sticking out.

The hunters crept onto the beach, unnoticed by the bear, and got out of the boat for the stalk. Fred had his 65-pound Kodiak

The following six photos are from a 35mm sequence camera showing Fred Bear arrowing a brown bear trophy with bow and arrow on the Alaskan Peninsula in May 1962. Above: Fred and his guide, Ed Bilderback, are hidden behind a rock as the bear approaches along water's edge.

recurve bow with four arrows tipped with Bear Razorheads. The guide and the photographer were armed with rifles in case back-up was needed. As they started the stalk, they were surprised to see the bear coming down the beach toward them. The photographer set up right where he was on the beach. Fred and the guide made their way closer to the bear to the only cover on the beach, a large rock. The bear continued to close the distance, ambling along at the water's edge. They waited. Finally, the bear came by at 25 feet, between the hunters and the water, where he paused to look over the rock and two objects. Satisfied, he turned broadside to walk on.

Fred drew and released the arrow. It sank to the feathers behind the front leg. The bear bellowed and headed down the beach straight for the photographer. The photographer stood his ground, taking pictures until the bear filled the frame of his camera, then he ran for cover. The mortally-wounded bear ran by him at full speed.

Brown bear continues along beach. Fred's arrow is ready to be drawn.

The big bear changes his course, sees the hunters and looks them over for a few seconds from 20 feet. Fred has his 65-pound Kodiak bow at nearly full draw.

The bear ignores the hunters. Bow fully drawn, Fred waits until the bear's front leg is forward to place the arrow behind it to enter the most vital area.

Fred releases the arrow and it strikes the bear. The arrow is buried to the feathers. The bear roars in rage and leaves in high gear.

The distance of the shot was 20 feet. The arrow penetrated completely and punched through the skin on the off side. The bear ran 90 yards.

Near the boat, the bear tried to get into an alder thicket, but died and rolled down to the water's edge. The arrow had hit a rib near the front leg, passed through a lung, cut an artery near the liver, then went through the diaphragm and through the skin near the ribs on the opposite side. He died in less than a minute, but covered 90 yards during his last seconds. The bear was weighed on scales by using the winch on the large boat Fred and his group were using as a base camp. It weighed 810 pounds. The hide squared nine feet, and the skull measured 27 inches.

This action was captured on film, and Bear Archery Company was kind enough to allow me to use the sequence in this book. It is visual proof that there is a place in big bear hunting for the properly-prepared bowhunter.

The first step for the bowhunter planning to hunt big bear is to obtain and learn the correct use of the proper equipment. Pete Shepley, President of Precision Shooting Equipment (PSE), is an experienced bowhunter for grizzlies and recommends the PSE Mach II Bow with an overdraw system set at 80 pounds. He matches this compound bow with XX75 Easton 2213 arrows, on which there are three-bladed Brute broadheads.

Fred Bear with his brown bear that squared nine feet. The skull measurement was 27 inches. Weight: 810 pounds. The razorhead arrow had done its job well. The bear lived less than 30 seconds after the arrow hit him.

Jim Dougherty, one of America's best-known bowhunters and bowhunting equipment experts, advises that no one should hunt large bear with a bow weight of under 60 pounds with a matching arrow of at least 500 grains to maximize penetration. He recommends conventional designs in broadheads, such as the Zwicky Black Diamond, Bear Razorhead, Magnus I or Magnus II. Dougherty points out that the heavy hair and fat layers on bear seriously impedes penetration, as well as working negatively on the cutting edge of the head.

I have shared a grizzly hunting camp with Dan Quillian, owner of Archery Traditions, a company that makes the traditional long bow. Dan recommends his Longhunter bow in the 70-pound class. He matches the bow with Easton 2419 arrows with feather fletchings and 190-grain, two-bladed Grizzly broadheads.

While the experts don't agree on brand names or types of bows, there are many things they do agree on. First and foremost is that you use a bow weight of over 60 pounds. The arrow you use

Pete Shepley with a grizzly he took using a Precision Shooting Equipment (PSE) bow.

must be matched to the bow. The broadhead should be tough enough not to come apart while traveling through the animal. And, *it must be razor sharp*! There is no excuse for a dull broadhead, and in the case of hunting big bear, it can be very dangerous.

You must practice before a bowhunt for bear until you can hit an exact point with your first shot, regardless of cold fingers, excitement or fear. Also, you must know exactly where on the bear your target is. You only have one shot, and it will probably be the most important single shot you will make during your bowhunting career. Pull a few inches one way or the other, and things may get exciting in a hurry. Practice makes perfect, and in this case, perfection is what you are after.

Putting the danger aside, just how important that one shot can be may be reflected in the success or failure of an expensive hunt. In 1966 when polar bear hunting was still permitted in Alaska, Fred Bear was hunting polar bear off the coast of Barrow on the pack ice. The hunt started April 13, and it was May 11 before a bear was sighted. Fred, the guide, and another hunter got in front of the bear's expected route and waited to ambush the slow-moving bear. They waited for 1½ hours in a pile of ice before they spotted the bear ambling their way. At a distance of a quarter mile, the bear changed his direction of travel. The hunters cautiously changed their location to cut the bear off. Now the bear was coming toward them, but it stopped at 50 yards out, sniffing and looking toward the hunters' ice cover. Fred decided this was going to be his only shot. He rose and shot. The arrow hit the bear behind the shoulder, and he went down, biting at the arrow in his side. Then, rising again, the bear started running over a pressure ridge; however, he had covered only 100 yards before he fell dead.

This one shot was all Fred got after 25 days of bad weather. It pays to have your act together if you plan to hunt big bear with a bow.

A few polar bear are still being taken by bowhunters. Jerome Knap of Canada North Outfitting, Inc. told me that he has had three American bowhunters on polar bear hunts during the past few years, and all three killed fine bear with shots within 25 yards.

Muzzleloading For Bear

The biggest surprise I got while researching this book was the difficult time I had finding hunters who had taken big bear with a muzzleloading rifle during modern times. Thanks to an appeal in the *North American Hunter* magazine, which asked NAHC members to contact me if they had accomplished this feat, I heard from several.

In 1977, NAHC member Keith Casteel, hunting with guide Gary Fait, took an 8-foot Alaskan grizzly with a .58 caliber flintlock using 150 grains of FFFG Blackpowder and a 500-grain original-type minie ball. He shot the grizzly at 70 yards. It took three well-placed shots to put the bear down for keeps.

I heard from Wesley Kyle of Pipe Creek, Texas, who took a brown bear on Kodiak Island in 1975 with a .58 caliber muzzleloader.

Fred Bear with a polar bear that he took in 1966 in Alaska.

NAHC member David Hofius with a grizzly that he took with his .54 percussion rifle.

NAHC member Harold Stocker of Sitka, Alaska, wrote that he took a brown bear on Chicagof Island using a Shiloh Sharps replica, .50-120 caliber, which has a falling block action and shoots blackpowder paper-patched bullets. At this writing, Stocker is planning another brown bear hunt on which he will be using a double rifle, the .58 caliber Kodiak II muzzleloader. He also plans to carry a .454 Casull revolver as a precaution.

John Y. Currie of Nome, Alaska, is another NAHC member who has taken a grizzly with a muzzleloader. John used the .58 caliber Kodiak Magnum double to take a 6½-foot blonde grizzly.

In 1978, NAHC member David Hofius of Cortland, Ohio, took a grizzly which had a 27-inch skull and squared 9½ feet. He used a .54 caliber percussion rifle.

Muzzleloading rifle hunters have several problems unique to their sport that can make bear hunting dangerous. The first problem is that muzzleloading rifles can be downright cranky about firing in the wet conditions in which a lot of bear hunting takes place. Next, when a bear is within 50 or so yards and the muzzleloading rifle hunter fires, he had better break the bear down. The noise, the cloud of white smoke and the sulfur smell of the burning powder help the bear pinpoint the hunter's location. Also, most muzzleloading rifles are one-shot firearms, with the reloading process taking about a minute. In the meantime, if the bear decides to charge, there is little that can be done but for you to let the guide finish the job you started.

Muzzleloading rifles that are best suited for large bear are .50 caliber or larger. It should fire its projectile with a muzzle velocity of a least 1,700 feet per second (fps) to get enough downrange energy to break a bear down in the shoulder.

The projectile you elect to use in the muzzleloading rifle should be selected with care. While there is no modern experience at hand to help guide the hunter into selecting the right ball or bullet, there is plenty of documentation from early explorers who encountered grizzlies regularly to know that round balls made of soft lead were not the best choice for putting the big bear down. In most cases, they depended upon several guns firing several times into a bear. Based on my studies of history and knowing something about what a bear can take and yet stay on his feet, I would rule out round balls.

There are now some lead conical bullets available to muzzleloading rifle hunters which have been giving excellent results on game such as elk, caribou and moose and would probably be sufficient on a grizzly in the hands of a skilled hunter. These are bullets made by Thompson/Center Arms Co. and Buffalo Bullet Co. The T/C Maxi-Ball is an accurate bullet in either 370-grain .50 caliber or 430-grain .54 caliber that has proven to have good penetration on black bear. The same can be said for Buffalo bullets, which are available in both .50 and .54 caliber, with bullet weights ranging from 385 grains to 460 grains.

Muzzleloading rifle hunters who have rifles with a 1:17 twist now have another option; by using a plastic sabot, they can use modern pistol bullets with controlled expansion. I have been shooting the Modern Muzzleloading Co. MK-85 .50 caliber rifle using Hornady .430-inch, 200-grain hollowpoint bullets in an MMP sabot over a 100-grain equivalent volume load of Pyrodex RS. This gives me two-inch groups at 100 yards with a muzzle velocity of 1,700 fps, plus deep penetration with a bullet that gives more controlled expansion than those made of soft lead.

A number of muzzleloading rifles are on today's market in the .50 and .54 caliber range that might be considered for big bear hunting. Since this is a game animal which usually requires more than one shot, double rifles, such as Connecticut Valley Arms' .50 caliber percussion Express Rifle or .50 caliber percussion Over/Under Rifle, might be a good choice.

I definitely suggest a rifle with a percussion ignition system over a flintlock system due to the wet conditions usually associated with bear hunting in the Far North.

Accessories that would be important to the muzzleloading rifle shooter hunting dangerous bear include a capper with plenty of caps in it tied around your neck so you could get to it in a hurry, and a coat pocket with several speed-load tubes in it. These plastic tubes have a pre-measured amount of powder in one end and a lubricated conical bullet in the other. It can speed up the reloading process greatly.

If I were going after a grizzly right now with a muzzleloading rifle, and I plan to do it soon, I would want a high-quality, percussion system .54 caliber double rifle with 1:17 twist barrels. On it I would have open adjustable sights with white outline rear sight and white front blade so they would function in low light conditions. I would choose a conical bullet that would give maximum controlled penetration. I would work on loads until I found one that would give me at least an 1,800 fps muzzle velocity. Then I would employ a guide who was good with a .338 Win. Mag.

Let The Guide Know

The best way to close this chapter is with some common-sense advice. Be sure to discuss the method you wish to hunt with your guide from the very beginning. After you have booked your hunt is the wrong time to spring the news on your guide that you plan to use a handgun, bow or muzzleloading rifle. The fact is that some guides don't want to take hunters who hunt with these devices. Some will take one, but not the other. Keep in mind that with the handgun, bow or muzzleloader, a lot of responsibility falls upon you to be skillful with its use and on your guide to be ready to possibly save your hide if things don't go well.

None of the guides I know want to go into the devil's club and alder thickets after a wounded bear, so don't be surprised if they make you prove you can shoot your handgun, bow or muzzleloader as well as you say you can. Be up-front about all your hunting plans when talking to your guide, and both of you will be glad in the end.

9

Shot Placement

Proper shot placement is important on all game, but it is more important on big bear than any other critter hunted in North America simply because a poorly-shot bear can bite back. I saw this demonstrated early in my hunting career many years ago while on a fall caribou hunt.

One of our hunters had a grizzly license he hoped to fill out. Early one morning, he and I were sitting on a steep tundra hill, glassing the vast valley below for caribou. I saw movement near the bottom of the same hill we were on, and when I put my glasses on it, I saw a grizzly plowing up a rockpile, digging for ground squirrels. The wind was blowing from the grizzly to us, so we began closing the distance to the busy bear.

The hunter with me had already demonstrated his shooting ability with his custom .300 Wthby Mag. back at the base camp. He could shoot a five-shot group at 100 yards that printed almost like one hole. We had talked at length, looking at a picture of a bear, about where he should hold on a grizzly to break the shoulders should we come upon one. We had also agreed that if he got an opportunity at a grizzly, he wouldn't stop shooting until the bear stopped moving.

Confident in the hunter's ability, I motioned for him to follow, and we went from alder patch to alder patch to get within shooting range of the bear. Near the end of our stalk, we ran out of cover and had to crawl to a depression that looked like a terrace in the side of the hill. When we got there, we were well-hidden and in a perfect position to look down the hill some 140 yards to where the unsuspecting bear was still trying to figure out how to catch a squirrel.

The hunter took off his jacket and rolled it up to rest his rifle on for a steady shot. I lay my rifle down and got on my belly to watch the bear through binoculars. The bear was broadside to us, giving the hunter a perfect shot.

It seemed like an hour went by before the Weatherby roared in my right ear. I heard the bullet strike the bear, but it sounded like it hit a drum. Howling, the bear spun around, biting itself in the side. Around and around he spun, still howling. The grizzly was obviously gutshot.

I waited for the second shot, but none came. Suddenly the bear stopped spinning, and with eyes fixed on me—eyes that looked afire—he started running up the steep slope, foam flowing from his mouth.

Time was critical now. I grabbed my rifle and shot. The bear took the hit in his chest and rolled to one side, but by the time I bolted in another round, he was getting up. I fired again, this time hitting his lower jaw with tremendous damage. He bawled and shook his head, slinging blood everywhere, and started moving in my direction again. This time I picked out his right shoulder and put a bullet in it. He fell and started rolling down the hill.

I bolted in my last round, hoping I wouldn't have to use it. But the bear caught the tundra in his claws, stopped rolling and, looking at me through a bloody face, pulled himself up again. This time, I put my final round under his now-destroyed chin. He sank to the ground, finished.

Now that the crisis was over, I realized two things: First, that the bear was just a few yards in front of me, and second, that my hunting companion—who never fired a second shot—was not beside me. Shaking and weak, I turned and saw him scrambling up the slope behind me as fast as he could go. It all made sense now. The bear probably never saw me. When the hunter realized he had made a bad first shot, he jumped up and started running up the slope. Then the gutshot bear saw the cause of all his misery and started running after it with revenge in his heart. I just happened to be in the middle.

This misadventure taught me a lesson that I will never forget about shot placement on a bear.

To understand why a big bear is so hard to put down for keeps, one must know something about the bear. First of all, the bear is at the top of the food chain and has been for centuries; therefore, it has no inherent fear of any living creature. When the first explorers came upon grizzlies, they were shocked at the animals' lack of fear. Grizzly, brown and polar bear still demonstrate this bold behavior.

Add to this lack of fear a degree of tenacity not seen in any other animal. Big bear have a will to live that is unequaled by any other creature and will fight to their last breath to survive. Wounds and injuries that would kill lesser animals often do not slow down the big bear.

Stories abound in the Far North about bear being shot, often repeatedly, only to be seen again the next year. One such bear made a name for himself in the panhandle of Alaska in the 1950s. This bear terrorized a river system with its loud roaring, enough to keep fishermen away from the river for years. When hunters finally killed the bear, the reason for its belligerence was found: a rifle bullet embedded in its skull next to the brain. The bullet, which had been shot into the bear years before, had fractured the skull, and the skull grew back into a grotesque shape. Such an injury would have killed most animals.

Another example of how much punishment a bear can take and go on living was related to me by Alaskan guide Bob Hannon. One of his bear hunting camps is near the village of Koyuk. A native fish camp in the area had been terrorized by a big bear for six years. Late each August, when the local fishermen were drying their fish on outdoor fish racks for the coming winter, the big bear would come into the camp and destroy two months' work in one night. This cut drastically into the family's winter food supply. The bear, which they called "The Rogue," knew no fear and would come into the camp to get the fish no matter what the consequences. He had been shot many times.

The local people asked Hannon to kill the bear for them, as they had suffered enough grief at the hands of this calculating raider. So Hannon moved his camp there and put one of his hunters on the bear, bringing its reign of terror to an almost anticlimactic end. On the second day of the hunt, the bear was quickly killed at 45 yards with a .338 Win. Mag. Browning semi-automatic BAR. The bear's hide squared 9 feet 3 inches, and the skull scored over 25 points.

But it wasn't until Hannon skinned the bear that he was sure they had taken "The Rogue." In skinning the bear, he found that the left front leg had a .22 bullet embedded in the wrist bone. The hams had been shot through with a high-powered rifle at one time, but the massive wound had healed up nicely. The entire face was carrying a load of No. 6 shot, and at some point, the bear had been shot in the face with 00 buckshot, as one of the pellets was lodged in the jaw where it had been broken and healed over. This wound alone meant that the bear probably didn't eat anything for about six weeks while the jaw was healing, a testament to just how tenacious a bear can be.

On top of his lack of fear and will to live, there is the awesome physical structure of a bear to contend with. He is built to withstand tremendous shock. An old Indian that I used to hunt with would say, "The griz is a ball of muscle and solid bone wrapped up in a tough skin." There's a lot of truth in that, and you really believe it when you skin and butcher one of the animals. Its bones, especially the small ones, are almost solid. They house little marrow. A meat saw has a tough time sawing through them. To this tough frame are tightly laced layer upon layer of massive muscles. Protecting that is a layer of fat. The outer layer is tough skin and thick hair. The shooter must shoot through all of that before he hits the vitals.

If the bear sees you, catches your scent, hears you or if anything else excites him at the moment you shoot, a charge of adrenaline is sent through his body that can keep him on his feet and moving unless hit in his spine or brain or his shoulders are badly broken. A wounded, super-charged bear that is still on his feet can pose a couple of perilous problems as long as life remains in his body. One, if he has a fix on you, he may charge. Two, if thick cover is nearby, he may run into the cover. This can be as frightening as having him run toward you, because now you have to go into thick brush after a wounded grizzly that may well be waiting for you, alive, angry and ready to pounce. This is a very important point to remember when hunting in country where cover is a leap away from the bear. The ideal situation is to shoot a totally unsuspecting bear that is calmly going about his business. It is this type of bear that hunters, especially bowhunters, take with one well-placed shot.

An example of what an excited grizzly can do and how hard he can be to put down was related to me by handgun hunter Larry Kelly, president of Mag-na-port International, Inc. While camping in a small shack on a river in Alaska, Kelly and his guide were

Larry Kelly shown with the brown bear that came into the cabin after him and his guide.

watching a grizzly feed along the river. When the bear saw the two hunters watching him, for no apparent reason, he started up the river bank at a fast pace in their direction. The guide fired two warning shots near the bear.

At the second shot, two things happened: the guide's rifle jammed, and the bear came in at a full run. The two hunters ran into the shack with the adrenaline-charged bear hot on their heels. As the bear came through the door, Kelly fired his Smith & Wesson Model 29 .44 Mag. revolver into the bear's chest at two feet. The bear spun around. Then the guide, with his rifle back in operation, began firing. When the bear finally gave up, the men had put 14 shots into its body. Kelly, who has killed big grizzlies with a handgun using only one shot, knows first-hand the difference between an unexcited bear with a normal flow of adrenaline and an excited bear that is super-charged by adrenaline.

Picking Your Shot

All of this has been said to lead up to the point of this chapter. Where should you hit a big bear to put it down as quickly, safely and humanely as possible?

Virtually every bear guide and experienced hunter I surveyed or have ever hunted with agrees that with a firearm, the first shot should strike the bear in the shoulder to break it and anchor the animal. This prevents a charge at the hunter and keeps the animal from reaching brush. The recommendation for subsequent shots varies among guides, but most prefer the second, third and fourth shot, if necessary, to be in the shoulder-lung area. A few guides like the second shot in the neck, provided the hunter is close to the animal and is a good marksman.

Contrary to what is sometimes written and discussed around campfires, the head or neck shot on a big bear is usually not a good idea. Either can be a tough target due to motion. The neck is short, and the only vital area in the neck is the spinal cord, which can be missed easily. If made properly, the head shot destroys the skull, and this is how bear are scored for trophy classing. This would be a poor place for a sportsman to shoot a bear, except in an emergency.

An improper head shot can tear away a chunk of the face, leaving you with one mad critter. When shooting at the head, anything short of a bullet in the brain is inadequate. While the head of a bear appears to be a sizable target, I have talked to a lot of old-time bear hunters who tell me about missing the head shot on

The head shot should be avoided except in an emergency.

bear as close as 25 yards. In short, forget the head shot unless there is no other option.

Several experienced bear guides I surveyed have a policy of continuing to shoot a bear in the vital area around the shoulder until it is down for keeps. Mark Meekin, a guide who has his hunting base near Palmer, Alaska, has the policy that his hunters make the first shot in the shoulder to put the bear down, and then keep shooting into the shoulder-lung area. He told me he has never had a close call with a bear one of his hunters shot, and trailing wounded bear is kept to a minimum. He adds, "A good taxidermist can patch up those holes."

The shoulder shot is relatively easy to take if the bear is standing broadside and the hunter has the presence of mind to take his time and pick his shot. An ideal hold is with the cross of the scope reticle on the center of the shoulder, with the vertical crosshair running up the center of the leg, provided the leg is in the usual all-fours standing position.

When the bear is quartering to or from the hunter, the shoulder shot requires a little more thought. If he is going away, hold in line

The zoo is a good place for imagining shot placement. The ideal hold on a broadside bear is at the center of the shoulder.

with the leg on the far side if it is in the normal standing position. If the leg is in the forward stepping position, hold along the rear of the leg. If the leg is in a rearward stepping position, hold along the front of the leg. If he is quartering to you, hold for the point of the shoulder.

The shoulder target is very small if the bear is facing you. When given a choice, the hunter should wait until the bear offers a broadside shot. Never pass up the opportunity to put a heavy, puncturing bullet through both shoulders if possible. Not only does it anchor the animal, but it often puts bone fragments into the lungs. If there is no choice and a head-on shot must be taken, the area to hit that will drop the bear is just to the right or left side of the bear's head. Shoot too far to the outside and you will only flesh-wound the bear; shoot too close to the center and you will hit the bear in the face.

Either will only infuriate the bear. Shooting the bear under the chin will put a bullet in the lungs or possibly the heart, which will kill him, but usually not on the spot. If his eyes are fixed on you,

When a bear is quartering away, hold in line with the leg on the far side.

the lungs or heart shot probably won't save you from the wrestling match of a lifetime.

An example of how a head-on shot can he effective if executed correctly was described to me by Mark Meekin. A sheep hunter he was guiding became very ill, and Meekin left the sheep camp at sundown to seek medical help. As darkness approached, he was making his way down a steep mountain trail as fast as he could when he almost ran head-on with a grizzly. Startled, the bear charged.

Meekin knew his first shot had better be good. He dropped to a kneeling position and held a sight picture on the bear's shoulder just beside the head. Due to the poor light and the bear's movement, the sight picture was difficult at best. The first shot broke the shoulder, spinning the bear around. Meekin emptied his rifle as fast as he could into the thrashing bear's lung area. When the dust cleared and the bear lay still, it was only 10 yards from where Meekin was kneeling. A miss of the shoulder on that first shot could have been fatal.

When a bear is quartering to you, hold on the point of the shoulder.

The so-called heart shot that some hunters talk about is a poor choice for a bear. The heart sits low in the bear's body and is a small, difficult target to hit. Heart shots on grizzlies wind up becoming brisket shots, and we're talking about a non-fatal wound that can make the job of searching for the wounded bear in the brush more adventure than you or your guide may want. Even if the shot is true, a bear can stay on his feet surprisingly long with his heart blown up. He is fatally wounded when the bullet strikes the heart, but he may not drop for a few minutes, allowing him to make his way into an alder thicket.

Don't take this shot. When a bear is facing you, wait until the animal turns to offer a shoulder shot.

The bottom line for gun hunters is to make every effort to make the first shot a well-placed shoulder shot, with follow-up shots in the shoulder-lung area, or in some situations, a neck shot. The hunter and guide should always discuss shot placement and what the hunter is to do after the first shot.

Bowhunters face an entirely different situation. They do not have the capability of breaking a big bear down. Their means of killing is to put a heavy, razor-sharp broadhead deep into the lungs, cutting vital arteries, veins and lung tissue. He must be backed by a guide with a rifle in case the bear locates them and decides to go to the source of the trouble.

The best shot for the bowhunter is just behind the front leg. To hit the shoulder or gut-shoot the bear can spell disaster. Most of the bowhunters I have talked to who have taken a big bear with a bow were surprised by how quickly the bear went down after taking the hit. However, I should point out that all of these hunters were expert shots and were shooting a bear that was calm and never knew what hit him. The bowhunter should avoid any shot other than the perfect lung shot at an unsuspecting bear within a reasonable range.

The late Fred Bear, who took as many big bear with a bow as anyone I know, told me that most bear, when hit with an arrow, will turn, howl, bite at the arrow, then run until they drop. In the same breath, however, Fred pointed out what most experienced bear hunters, guides and biologists know: each bear is different and you can't predict what a bear will do.

It is a common misconception that bear are generally seen standing upright. We have all seen movies and illustrations of ferocious grizzlies charging in an upright position. I have even seen a magazine article showing where to shoot the upright, charging grizzly. The truth of the matter is that bear spend little time walking around on their hind legs like a man. They will stand erect if they are trying to see over vegetation or feeding on or trying to reach something high, but most of the bear you will see or shoot will be on all fours. I have only seen one bear shot standing, and that was a large black bear my wife shot in some dark timber along the British Columbia coast. This bear was not charging, but seemed simply curious about what was in the brush with him.

Chances are, you won't have to make a shot at an upright bear, but if you do, break him down in the shoulders with a rifle or handgun, or put an arrow through his heart and lungs if bowhunting.

Practicing Shot Placement

Reading about shot placement on an 800- to 1,200-pound bear is one thing, but actually having the self-discipline to pick out a one-square-inch target on the side of a hairy beast half the size of a pickup truck is quite another. Most guides agree that the mistake that causes most bear hunts to become a blood-trailing adventure is the hunter's inability to hit the "sweet spot." They aim their rifle, handgun or bow at the middle of the critter and let go.

The first thing that the hunter planning a bear hunt should do is study the anatomy of a bear. Memorize the physique of a bear so

Alaskan big bear guide Mark Meekin, above, advises hunters to keep shooting at the shoulder/lung area until the bear is down for keeps.

that you know the location of the bony structure of the shoulders, the lungs and the heart. Next, you need to look at some life-size bear to study exactly where you would shoot. The best place to do this is at a zoo. Many zoos throughout the country have both grizzly and polar bear that you can watch. If a black bear is all that is available, watch him. Use binoculars to pick out shoulder or lung shots as the bear stands and walks at different angles.

Most guides say that it is much easier to work with hunters who have studied live bear than with a hunter who is seeing his first bear through a riflescope on a tundra slope. Once you begin to feel comfortable at picking out the target area on zoo bear, get some bear targets to use on the range.

Several archery supply companies and other target companies sell reasonably-priced bear targets. Take these targets out to your range and practice shooting the same equipment you plan on shooting on your hunt, at the same distances you may be shooting at while hunting. Practice shooting at the right spot.

Continue your practice in failing light, and shoot from the positions you may have to use on your bear hunt. In the case of rifle shooting, use a tight sling and shoot from a standing, sitting and kneeling position. Shoot from a rest, such as a post or tree. Concentrate on making first shots that would break the bear's shoulder. The handgun hunter and bowhunter will want to spend the same amount of time on his shooting positions. Regardless of what you hunt bear with, the bear targets will force you to pick your point, making you proficient at shot placement.

You can never practice too much.

10

Dealing With
The Wounded Bear

Less than half a mile from our base camp, a hunter had become too excited and, not listening to his guide, had put two rounds from his .338 Win. Mag. through a big grizzly's rear end. The enraged bear had made it into a thick patch of alders about half the size of a city block. The guide had made two attempts to get the hunter into the alders to finish what he had started, but the roaring and thrashing of bushes from within the heart of the thicket had caused them to retreat. This commotion had taken place early in the morning, so they returned to camp for coffee and a plan of attack.

When I heard this story, I was disappointed in the hunter for making a poor shot and in the guide for leaving the alder thicket. "What if the bear leaves the thicket while you are here?" I asked. "The last thing we need around here is a gut-shot bear."

Along with the camp cook, we returned to the alder thicket, now quiet except for the rustle of bushes as a gust of wind blew. The hunter, with his guide at his side, took up a position on a high bank to the east of the thicket. If the bear was still in the jungle and came out, they could get a shot on three sides.

I eased around the edge of the alders with the cook, who was an excellent hunter, trying to cut sign to see if the bear had come out. It was hard to constantly look down, knowing that the bear might break out of the alders at any moment. We could find no exit at all. If we were lucky, he was still in there.

Assuming he was, we decided the cook would get into a position on the west side of the alder thicket where he could get a shot if the bear made an escape in that direction. Hoping the shot was better than I had been told and that the bear had bled to death, I told the others I would ease into the thicket from the south with the wind in my face. I checked my rifle like a soldier about to go into combat and studied the southern edge of the alders.

A washed-out gully about three feet deep ran through the thicket from north to south. Since the alders were not so thick there and I felt that I could move in the gully quietly, I decided to explore the thicket along that path.

As I started up the gully with my rifle in a ready position and my thumb on the safety, I noticed how quiet it was. I slowly eased my way up the uneven gully, pushing past alder limbs that seemed to be grabbing for me, stopping every few steps to stoop so that I could see along the ground. It was more open at this low level, and I hoped to see the bear, assuming he was still there, long before he saw me.

I had been in the thicket for about 15 minutes and had gone about 75 yards up the gully when to my left front, a dark mass lunged into the bushes just above me. I jumped back, shouldering my rifle and flipping off the safety. The mass let out a deafening roar that sent a chill through my crouched body. He was only 20 feet away, and I was certain his next lunge would put him right on top of me, but I couldn't see enough of the bear to pick out a vital spot. He clicked his teeth loudly and roared again. The bushes were thrashing and I was expecting the worst.

Suddenly, I saw the big head looking straight at me just about a foot off the ground. I held the .375 H&H Mag. on his chin and fired once, then a second quick shot. All was deathly quiet again. I strained my eyes for movement, but the bear was still. The big bullets had found their mark.

I sat there for a while waiting for the others to join me. It was then that I realized just how badly that bear had wanted me. If he hadn't been broken down from the hunter's shots, that gully would have been full of bear.

That was my first experience with a wounded bear. It taught me the seriousness of the matter and just how vital it is to put a bear down with the first shot.

All guides agree that the first rule when hunting big bear is to not wound one if gun hunting. If bowhunting, you must stick an arrow in a vital area without the bear ever knowing you are there and carefully watch his exit, because you will have to follow him later. A wounded bear is the most unpredictable animal on earth and can be the most dangerous. Even when they are down, you can't be too cautious. My good friend Charlie Elliot, who for many years thrilled the readers of *Outdoor Life* magazine with his adventures, once told me about a grizzly he shot in Alaska. Wounded, the bear went into a wallow under some alders.

Charlie shot the bear a second time, and the bear rolled into the bushes and collapsed. To make sure he was dead, the guide Charlie was hunting with tossed a stone at the grizzly's head. The bear jumped up and charged the two surprised hunters with a roar. Charlie said it was so loud it shook the ground.

The guide, who did not have his rifle with him, thought Charlie wasn't prepared to shoot again, so he took off up the mountain with the bear after him. Just as Charlie was about to shoot again, the bear, weak from his wounds, ran back under the alders. Charlie shot it in the head. This time, they left the now-silent bear to go back down the mountain and help a second hunter skin out a bear he had taken. It would give them an opportunity to get over the scare Charlie's bear had given them.

They skinned out the bear, and the guide sent the two hunters with the hide and skull down to the horses while he took Charlie's rifle with a couple of cartridges up to skin Charlie's bear.

The guide cautiously walked up to the fallen grizzly when it stood up and lunged at him! The guide shot the bear in the chest and took off down the mountain, bolting the rifle with the bear on his heels, swinging its paws at him. The guide fired his second and last round over his shoulder at point-blank range. Lucky for him, this bullet broke the big grizzly's back, killing it.

I use this story to illustrate that big bear can take a lot of punishment and keep coming back for more, often when you think it's over. Most of the guides I've hunted with have a policy of putting a last bullet into the neck or spine of a big bear, even when he appears very dead.

What do you do when you have hit a big bear that stays on his feet and makes it into thick cover?

Rule Number One: *Do exactly what your guide tells you to do.* You are paying him good money for his experience and knowledge, and this would be a foolish time not to follow his instructions. After all, he has probably faced this situation several times and knows what to do.

Next, be able to call your shots. Where did you hit the bear? How did he react as he ran off? Where did you last see him? The answers to these questions will help you and your guide determine a course of action.

Be sure to reload your rifle or handgun and put the safety on "Safe."

The third step is one all guides recommend. Wait! Give the bear an hour or so to settle down and, hopefully, die. This is difficult for some hunters to do, but it is a critical follow-up step. If the bear is critically wounded, it won't go far. Immediate pursuit will only keep him running or create a dangerous situation for the hunter. What happens after that varies from guide to guide.

Based on the terrain, weather, shot placement, skill of the hunter and many other factors, each will plan the effort to get your bear as the situation dictates. Tom Rigden, a guide with Mountain Enterprises Guide Service, and one with whom I've enjoyed hunting, follows these steps after waiting an appropriate length of time:

1) Rigden situates the hunter so he can see the guide and the area where the bear was last seen. As Rigden enters the brush, he makes sure the hunter is watching so he can alert the guide if he sees the bear.

2) When following a blood trail, Rigden constantly watches the surrounding brush, since bear are known to circle their quarry and attack from the rear.

3) If the hunter has to follow Rigden into the brush, the guide has him walk several steps behind or to one side with his rifle on "Safe," so as to create two distinct lanes of fire should the bear be encountered.

4) After the bear is located, dead or alive, Rigden or his hunter shoots it again to make sure. Then the guide approaches the bear with the hunter standing off to one side, ready to fire if necessary.

Rigden is quick to point out that no two bear respond exactly alike when wounded, so the hunter has to expect anything. He had a heart-stopping hunt during the 1987 bear season when he was guiding a hunter for bear on the Alaskan Peninsula. Scouting revealed that a bear was feeding on a moose kill from a previous hunt. Rigden cut shooting paths in the bush around the kill so various approaches could be made to the kill, depending upon the wind conditions.

When following a wounded bear, do exactly as your guide says. Lots of things, including your own safety, depend on it.

When the bear showed up again on the kill, Rigden moved his hunter to within 50 yards of the bear. With the hunter in position, Rigden began kicking brush with his feet to get the bear to move and give the hunter a better shot. The bear stood up, and the hunter fired his Wthby .340 Mag., knocking it down. With a frightening roar, the bear got up and was shot a second time. Again he went down, but got up and ran parallel to the hunters into thick alders and cottonwoods. They waited an hour before following the bear into the dense thicket.

For a while they had a good blood trail to follow, but after a three-quarter-mile stalk, the trail ran out. Rigden realized they were playing a cat-and-mouse game with no appreciable gain, so they decided to return to camp and regroup the next morning with Mountain Enterprises chief guide Brad Langvardt.

The next morning, they found a faint blood trail where they had stopped the afternoon before. The two guides spent a painstaking six hours turning over leaves, looking for the tiniest blood drop.

They had broken into a small clearing when Rigden saw a hawk land in a bush about 150 yards away. Thinking the bird might possibly be feeding on the bear carcass, he headed toward it, leaving Langvardt at the blood trail. Rigden hadn't walked 25 yards in the chest-high willows when he heard the bear roar off to his right. Shouting to Langvardt that he had heard the bear, he brought his rifle to his shoulder.

At that moment, the bear appeared at fifteen yards, staring straight at Rigden. He fired, hitting the bear just below the chin. Langvardt, only about 25 yards from the bear, also shot it, this time through the shoulders. At last, the bear was finished. This tough old bear's hide squared 10 feet 2 inches, and the skull measured 28³⁄₁₆.

Alaskan guide Bob Hannon emphasized to me that the major reason for bear being wounded is hunters shooting at ranges greater than 100 yards. He is a firm believer in getting as close as reasonably possible to shoot.

During the 15 years he has been guiding bear hunters, Hannon has had only eight bear wounded; just one of those got away. While he's waiting at least 45 minutes, he makes sure his rifle muzzle is free of snow, mud and other obstructions and that it is properly loaded and working. Then he positions his hunter out of the brush and uses one or two guides to follow the blood trail. He puts one guide up front to ease along ahead of the second guide,

Guide Tom Rigden makes decisions about blood-trailing a wounded bear based on terrain, weather, shot placement and skill of the hunter.

who blood trails, and to keep a sharp look out for any sign of movement or any sound of the bear. Often on a quiet day, a wounded bear can be heard licking his wounds and even breathing. Hannon spaces his trailers out five to six feet apart to keep a charging bear from hitting more than one man.

Hannon's closest call with a wounded grizzly came when a hunter shot a bear in the hind quarter. The bear was in a creek bed adjacent to some thick willows. The hunters on a high bank could see the willows moving and hear the bear clicking his teeth just inside the brush. After a wait, Hannon positioned his hunter on top of the high bank and proceeded to climb down into the creek bottom. Instead, he fell down the bank and rolled up to the edge of the willows. As he stopped falling, the willows next to him shook and roared. He shot three times at point-blank range. Quickly he reloaded, as the bear tried to get through the brush at him. Hannon peered through the thrashing brush and finally made out the head and neck at six feet. He shot the bear in the neck, killing it. Afterward, he learned why the bear never got him; it was broken down too badly in the hind quarters. Hannon understates, "That was some bear hunt."

Sometimes a wounded grizzly doesn't give hunters time to follow good blood-trailing practices. In 1986, Cy Ford, a British Columbia guide with whom I've hunted, had two bear hunters in a 20-foot aluminum river boat searching for grizzlies on the Kitlope River. Near the Kitlope confluence with the Tsaytus River, they spotted a lone grizzly walking along the bank of a side channel. Leaving one hunter with the boat, Ford took the other hunter to try to get close to the bear. At 200 yards, they saw they could get no closer. They decided to give it a try. Ford advised the hunter to wait until he had a broadside shot at the shoulder. When the grizzly turned to his right, Ford told the hunter to shoot. Just as the .300 Win. Mag. went off, the grizzly suddenly changed directions, and Ford saw the bullet hit the bear's hind leg. The grizzly went down, wallowing on the ground and bellowing madly. The hunter fired two more rounds, but Ford couldn't tell if they hit the bear. At the third shot, the bear got up and ran into the bush.

Ford then walked along the channel looking for a shallow place to wade across; the hunter followed. Just across the channel was a large patch of cottonwood trees into which the bear had disappeared at the upper end. As Ford approached opposite the lower end of the cottonwoods, he saw the grizzly in a full charge coming right for him, quickly closing the 40-foot span. The hunter fired, but the bear continued. Ford threw up his Ruger .338 Win. Mag. and fired as the bear splashed across the channel with eyes fixed on him. The 250-grain Nosler Partition hit the bear under the chin, entering the chest cavity. Falling over backwards from the shot, he drifted with the current and lodged completely under water below a log hanging off the bank.

After the dead bear was retrieved, Ford found that the hunter had hit the bear twice. Although there was a lot of blood, the grizzly hadn't been seriously hurt; it apparently felt that Ford was the cause of his aggravation and intended to do him in.

Alaska guide Larry Rivers is another believer that anything can

British Columbia guide Cy Ford has had plenty of experiences going after wounded bear.

happen when following a wounded bear. He was guiding a hunter who shot and wounded a brown bear on the coast of Alaska. They followed the wounded bear at a long distance along the rocky beach, keeping the animal in sight. Then the bear came to a high rock outcrop that blocked the beach, and he swam out into the ocean and around the rock. The hunters were unable to follow.

Disappointed, they had to abandon the bear. They started walking back along the beach to camp, but they hadn't walked far when they heard gravel falling from a high rock cliff above them. They looked up to see another brown bear some 20 feet above them. The bear charged and the hunter fired. The dead bear fell to the beach, knocking the two big-eyed men sprawling. It happened in a matter of seconds.

The bowhunter is the most vulnerable to problems from wounded bear, since the arrow kills by hemorrhaging and doesn't usually knock a bear right down. Most successful bowhunters have to deal with a potentially still-alive bear that hasn't bled to death yet.

Jake Jacobsen, master guide and owner of Arctic Rivers Guide Service in Alaska, shared a close-call bowhunt with me. In 1981, Jacobsen had a five-day period during which his hunting clients were delayed. He and his wife watched three big caribou bulls swim across the river near their base camp. As the bulls stood on the opposite bank shaking the water off, a big grizzly rushed out of the willows and knocked one of the bulls down. It never returned to its feet. The grizzly dragged the bull into the dense willow brush.

Later that day Jacobsen flew out of camp for supplies. The next day, while preparing to land his plane back at the base camp, he saw the big grizzly sitting on his kill with two more grizzlies nearby. That evening he decided to try to take the big bear with his bow. He had taken caribou with a bow and figured if he could get within 25 to 30 yards of the grizzly, he would have a good chance. His wife would back him up with her rifle, and he would carry a 12 gauge, .30-06 drilling slung on his back in case all else failed.

The next morning, Jacobsen and his wife started the stalk. When they got close to the caribou kill, Jacobsen told his wife to chamber a round and get ready to shoot if he yelled. He was counting on the bear being asleep, since he was full and wolves had barked and yipped around the kill all night.

But the bear was awake and saw the duo before they saw him. Without making a sound, the bear came at them on the run.

The faintest blood trail is easy to follow in snow, and the crippled bear has a tough time getting away in deep snow.

Jacobsen said the first thing he saw was the pink inside of the bear's nose. This experienced bear hunter had an overwhelming feeling that there was going to be an accident. By reflex he drew back the bow and released the arrow. It hit the bear in the base of the neck at an angle and penetrated to four inches from the fletching. He later learned that the broadhead had severed some major arteries and lodged in a lung.

The grizzly turned from his charge and tried to bite the arrow. Jake stuck him with a second arrow; however, it was a poor hit, as he had overdrawn. Not only that, but the overdraw cut his index finger and thumb badly, right through his glove. His wife hollered, "Jake, let's get outta here!" With his hand bleeding profusely and the grizzly thrashing wildly, he was now expecting the worst.

Dropping the bow, he shouldered the drilling. The grizzly continued to thrash about for a minute, biting at the first arrow—then fell over dead. His charge had been stopped at less than 16 feet. Had the wound been any less serious, the outcome may have been much different. This wounded bear didn't die any too soon.

The bear placed sixth in the Pope & Young record book.

Through the 1987 season, Jacobsen had been in on the killing of 151 bear, either as hunter or guide, and had only been charged 12 times. Of these, eight were wounded bear, two were grizzlies on kills, one was a sow with cubs and one was unprovoked.

There is no precise procedure for blood-trailing a wounded bear, as there is for whitetail deer. I have seen bear that lost a good bit of blood survive without any difficulty and some which lost little blood but were found dead. The fat and long hair on the bear often cause the blood trail to be faint.

Guides who hunt most of their bear when snow is on the ground seem to have the best percentage of recovering wounded bear. The faintest blood trail is easy to follow, and the crippled bear has a tough time getting away in deep snow.

The potential danger of trailing a wounded bear cannot be over-emphasized. I have talked to the survivors of two wounded-bear hunts in which the bear killed one of the hunters, and it was a tragedy for both the victim and the survivors.

Many dead bear have been found in a position which afforded them an ambush should anyone have been on their backtrail. Their last instinct was to confront the cause of their pain.

There should never be a bear wounded and lost by a modern rifle or handgun hunter. If the big bear hunter will work hard to get

Good hunting techniques and good marksmanship can prevent the necessity of blood-trailing a wounded bear.

within 100 yards of an unsuspecting bear, pick his target well and place his shot through the shoulders, the bear will be anchored. Then the second and, if necessary, third shots should be driven through the shoulder/lung area. As Larry Rivers puts it, ''There should be no one-shot bear.'' This is not the time for an ego trip.

If the bear is wounded or if you hunt with a bow or muzzleloading rifle where death may not be instant, these rules should be followed:

1) Reload immediately.
2) Check your rifle barrel with the bolt open to be sure there's no obstruction.
3) Be sure your firearm's action is working properly and is properly loaded.
4) Wait! Give the bear 45 minutes to one hour to die or settle down. Be quiet and alert during this wait.
5) While waiting, analyze your shot placement, the bear's reaction and exit route.
6) When the blood-trailing begins, have at least two armed hunters involved, one to watch and listen while the other follows the blood trail.
7) Stay at least six feet apart in case of a charge.
8) Be ready for anything.
9) Don't take chances. Big bear are dangerous, and rushing the trailing of a wounded bear is a mistake.

11

Avoiding
Bear Problems

This might seem like a strange chapter in a book that is devoted to the locating and stalking of bear, but it is a necessary chapter. Most bear-caused deaths and maulings do not occur when the hunter shoots a bear; they usually occur in camp or when people are walking in big bear country. One of the most publicized bear maulings occurred in 1971 when Alaska game warden Al Thompson and his wife backpacked into the Kenai National Moose Range to bowhunt for moose. Thompson also carried his .44 Mag. handgun, and his wife took her .30-06.

Their camp was a comfortable lean-to made of poles and plastic.

On the second night of their hunt, Thompson was awakened at 3:30 a.m. by a sense that something was wrong. He woke his wife and told her to stay still, something was outside. As Thompson reached for the rifle, an enraged grizzly came through the top of the lean-to. Knocking the rifle from Thompson's hand, the bear began trying to tear Mrs. Thompson from her sleeping bag. Thompson hit the bear with his hand, and the bear turned on him. There was no time to grab the pistol. The bear snatched his left arm and flung him across the lean-to. Next, it grabbed Thompson's scalp with its mouth, picking him up, and ran out of the lean-to. The bear's front paw ripped a gash in Thompson's chest.

After carrying Thompson 80 feet, the bear dropped him.

Thompson knew that he would have to play dead with his belly down if he was to survive. His left arm useless, he used his right arm to position himself belly down and held his breath until he almost passed out. The bear chewed on Thompson's back and hit the side of his head with his claws as the man played dead. Abruptly, the bear left.

The rest of the story is a credit to both Thompson and his wife, as they had to walk out some 15 miles to get help. Thompson survived, but it was a long battle to recovery.

Alaskan guide Larry Rivers tells two interesting accounts of bear coming into hunting camps. Once his wife heard their dog barking, and she stepped out of the cook tent to see the dog half in and half out of the family tent, where their daughter was asleep. The dog was barking at a grizzly only about three yards away. Mrs. Rivers picked up some stones and threw them at the bear. The bear ran out of camp down to the edge of a nearby river, where he proceeded to consume the groceries that were in the river to be kept cool. Next, the bear stomped up and down the river's edge. Then the bear charged back into camp and Mrs. Rivers, with shotgun in hand, threw a stick at the bear, causing him to run back to the river. Reaching the river, the bear turned and once again charged into camp straight at Mrs. Rivers. She was forced to shoot when the bear got within 20 feet. One charge of 00 buckshot killed the bear.

On another occasion, Rivers had two guides and two hunters in a spike camp, which had a four-man tent suspended from an exterior frame with elastic cord. One night a brown bear sow with three cubs came into camp and rather enjoyed, much to the horror of the tent's occupants, putting their feet up on the tent, pushing it down, and then letting it spring back up. This went on for two to three hours. Once a cub annoyed its mother, and she slapped it into the tent's side. At daybreak, one of the guides unzipped the tent door some four inches at the bottom to look out. As he bent down to look out, with the other three hunters also trying to get a peek, the sow stuck her nose through the opening. Instantly, the previously-crowded tent had plenty of room around the door.

Soon after that, the bear left them and the hunters moved their camp about a quarter mile, hoping to have some peace that night.

But it was not to be, as that night, the same bear came into the new campsite to play with the tent again. This time, one of the guides decided to shoot his .338 Win. Mag. with the muzzle next to the sow's head in hopes it would scare the bear away. Sticking

Bear camps should be set up away from bear trails and feeding areas to avoid an unwanted confrontation.

the rifle barrel only 18 inches away from the sow's head, the guide fired into the air. The old sow never blinked an eye. Once again, the bear started playing on the tent. It was another long night.

The first rule in avoiding bear problems in camp is to not set up camp in a place that forces bear to move through a small area. Don't set up camp on or adjacent to a bear trail. Avoid sites where roaring streams drown out sounds; bear that hear you will usually avoid you. Also, don't camp near bear feeding sites, such as berry patches and salmon spawning areas.

Be sure to plan your camp carefully, especially if it is a base camp. Keep sleeping tents together, separate from the kitchen and food storage areas. The sleeping tent should be upwind of the cook tent. Evening winds usually blow down valley. Clear out all underbrush and branches around camp below four or five feet for better visibility along the ground.

Perhaps the most important rule is to make all food storage bear-proof, either by suspending it from a tree out of reach of bear or in food storage containers made from metal drums.

One of the most frightening nights I ever spent in a hunting camp was in a camp with cabins made from logs with a tent top. There were two cabins in camp: a cook cabin with a large picnic table in it, where all cooking and eating took place, and a sleeping cabin, where guides and hunters slept. Since the cook had to get up so early each morning to prepare breakfast on time, he slept on the large table in the cook cabin.

One night we were all awakened by the sound of splintering wood and the cook screaming. Then there were five shots from the cook cabin. The cook hollered for us not to come out, that a bear had torn the door off its hinges and gotten in the cabin with him. The cook, who had managed to leap off the table while still in his sleeping bag, had grabbed a shotgun loaded with slugs and emptied it into the bear at arm's length.

We shined a bright flashlight over on the cook tent doorway to see the big-eyed cook sticking his head out, trying to reload the shotgun. No one slept, thinking the wounded bear was just outside our camp. The next morning, we found the bear dead a few yards from the cook tent.

Keeping a clean camp can go a long way toward avoiding bear trouble. All dishes should be washed after meals. Food garbage should be burned. Horse pellets and strong-smelling plastics and lubricants should be stored like food and away from camp. Day packs should be checked when returning to camp to discard food leftovers.

I credit a clean camp for preventing another hunter and me from having major bear problems. We were stranded near the Yukon-British Columbia line with little camp gear except our two-man mountain tent and sleeping bags. The only food we had for days was trout we caught from the lake where our survival camp was located. Bear sign was all around, and we took great pains to sink all trout scraps, including the sticks we cooked them on, out in the lake. It was a good thing, for each night a grizzly would come into camp, even with a campfire burning near the door of our small tent, and sniff around the tent. It was awesome to lie in the tent and see its sides shake from the bear's breath and hear him sniff all around the edges. He never caused a problem other than a loss of sleep.

One way you can keep most bear out of camp is to urinate at different locations around the camp. Of course, this can foul up your hunting around the camp, especially downwind.

When camping in small tents, it is a good idea to keep a sharp

Food should be stored well out of reach of bear, such as in a cache.

knife handy so that you can create a door if necessary. Also, it's wise in any camp to keep a bright flashlight and your rifle handy. Some grizzly and brown bear guides keep dogs in camp as an early warning of bear. The sled dogs used on polar bear hunts serve this same purpose.

Always carry your rifle with you when leaving the immediate camp area to go down to a stream, to take a hike or to go to the bathroom.

Be sure to hang game meat out of the reach of bear.

If you are hiking around camp, be sure to make plenty of noise so as not to surprise a bear. All bear have a certain "critical space." If you surprise a bear within that range, anything can happen. Don't try to slip up on a bear to take photographs, or worse yet, feed the bear. Enter thickets from upwind so your smell will warn bear of your presence.

If you should encounter a bear, stay calm, as it will probably leave you alone once it gets your scent. Don't make abrupt moves or noises that would startle the bear. Give it plenty of room. Slowly detour, keeping upwind so it will get your scent and know you are there. If you cannot detour, look for a tree to climb while waiting for the bear to move away. Most grizzlies won't climb a tree after you, but some have been known to climb right behind a man if the limbs are close together. Most bear don't charge, but some will, sometimes for no apparent reason. If one should charge, your options are:

1) Climb a stout tree.

2) Drop a pack or coat to distract the bear while you ease off.

3) Shoot the bear, making sure your first shot either breaks his shoulders or enters the brain.

4) If unarmed, assume a cannonball position to protect your head and stomach while playing dead.

The one option you don't have is to run. Amazing as it may seem, big bear can attain a burst of speed up to 40 miles per hour in seconds. Also, it is instinctive for them to chase running animals.

As has been reiterated over and over in this book, big bear are unpredictable. Their reasons for attacking are many. A bear may attack if it considers you a threat. A polar bear may consider you a meal. You may get too close to a bear or to cubs, startle it or run up on a bear that has been beaten by another bear or had a previous run-in with men. It could be injured, or it could just be one of those attacks for which there is no apparent explanation.

Since, in all likelihood, your bear hunts and most other hunts conducted in big bear country will be guided, you will be under the watchful eye of a professional who knows how to avoid bear problems. By following his rules, you probably won't have any trouble.

More outdoorsmen are hurt and killed each year by poisonous snakes, lightning and many other acts of nature than by all bear, so the risk is not great *if* you take some precautions.

12

Trophy Bear

A ny legally-harvested polar, grizzly or brown bear is certainly a trophy to the hunter who brings the animal down in a sporting manner. Due to the nature of big bear hunting, we don't always have the opportunity to pick and choose our bear. However, most of us would like to take a bear that is really considered big. In many cases, it is simply luck if a trophy-sized bear is taken, but sometimes other factors come together and give you the opportunity to look at several bear from which to choose.

Field Judging

Big bear are among the most difficult animals to judge in the field. To most hunters, they all look big. Alaska guide Larry Rivers tells me there is no substitute for experience in field-judging bear. He and his assistant guides study the valleys they hunt in and learn the size of reference points, such as cut banks, rocks, etc. Then when they see a bear out at a distance, they compare it in size to one of the known reference points at a similar distance.

In open country, it is even harder to judge the distance. Is it a big bear far away or a small bear fairly close? For accurate distance judging, a rangefinder can be helpful.

If he is tracking a bear, Rivers measures the distance across the pad of one of the bear's front feet in the tracks. To that he adds one inch. That measurement in inches is generally equal to the feet the

When field-judging bear, remember that really big bear look big. Also, very large bear walk with a swinging waddle.

bear's hide will square. This doesn't hold true all the time, but it's a good rule of thumb to use in the field. For instance, if the bear's footprint is seven inches across the pad, the bear hide will probably square around eight feet.

Rivers also points out that if you ask yourself, "I wonder if that's a big bear?" when watching a bear, he probably isn't very big, but if your initial reaction is "That's a huge bear," he probably is. Big bear look big to those who have seen a few bear.

Other rules of thumb used by guides when judging bear include one which considers how the bear walks. Very large bear walk with a swinging waddle, and small bear walk with no waddle or movement in the rear. Some guides say they judge a bear by its legs. If they appear to be very short with the body close to the ground, it is a large bear. If the legs appear to be long with the body high, it is a small bear.

Guide David O'Keeffe describes a large bear as looking like a mule without legs. A guide I worked with in British Columbia judges his bear by their ears; if they appear to be small and stick

Fred Bear with his then-world-record brown bear shot in 1960.

out of the side of the head, it is usually a large bear. If the ears are easily seen and stick out the top of the head, it is a small bear.

Since chances are good you will be hunting with a guide who knows what a really big bear looks like, you won't have to know any special tricks for field-judging bear. Unfortunately, many hunters do not find enough bear to be too picky. It takes luck to get a high-scoring bear.

Squaring The Hide

Harvested bear are evaluated in two ways: by "squaring" the hide and by measuring the skull.

The paw of Fred Bear's 1960, then-world-record brown bear.

To square a hide, first lay the fresh skin out flat. Using a measuring tape, measure from the end of its nose to the end of its tail, not counting hair. Then, without moving the hide, measure from the end of the claws on one front foot to the end of the claws on the other front foot. Add the two measurements and divide the total by two. You have the square measurement.

Big inland grizzlies will square up to eight feet or so, coastal grizzlies and browns will square up to about 10 feet, and polar bear up to about 11 feet. A brown or grizzly hide may be as wide as it is long, while a polar bear hide is long and narrow.

You can see that this is a general method of earning bragging rights, and the unscrupulous guide or hunter can easily stretch the green hide to obtain exaggerated numbers. I once watched two hunters pull and tug on a green grizzly hide to get a high squared measurement to the point of almost pulling off one of the front legs where several bullets had hit the bear. If done correctly, squaring is a good method of sizing up a bear.

A black bear skull (left) looks small compared to that of a grizzly.

Measuring The Skull

The method of scoring a trophy bear that is accepted by most trophy records programs is measuring a clean, dry skull. Notice I said "clean and dry." All flesh, cartilage and membrane must be off the skull and the skull allowed to dry for at least 60 days.

A caliper is needed to measure the skull. Two measurements are taken with the caliper, each to the nearest one-sixteenth of an inch. The first measurement is the longest length, from the forward tip of the skull to the rear of the skull. The second measurement is the widest point of the skull. These two measurements are added to give the score.

Not only is the skull a means of trophy scoring, but a bleached skull on a plaque makes a nice trophy display.

Several hunting organizations have hunter recognition awards for hunters taking trophy-class bear.

Boone & Crockett Club

The best known and most prestigious recognition comes from the Boone & Crockett Club. They have been keeping a record book

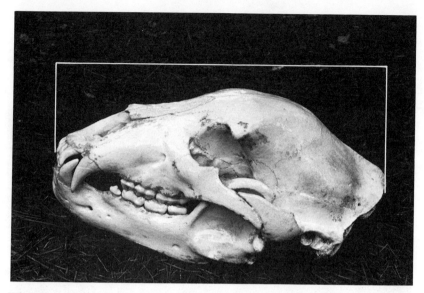

When determining the size of the skull, the length of the bear's skull is included.

on North American big game since 1932, and most of us hunters would like to have a trophy animal "in the book," a term referring to the Boone & Crockett Club record book. Their scoring techniques are simple and fair and are used by many other organizations for trophy rating. The Boone & Crockett Club only accepts the measurements of one of its trained official measurers.

For their record book, the Boone & Crockett Club has a separate category for the big coastal brown bear and the interior grizzly. A line of separation between the larger-growing coastal brown bear and the smaller interior grizzly has been developed such that west and south of this line (to and including Unimak Island), bear trophies are recorded as Alaska brown bear. North and east of this line, bear trophies are recorded as grizzly bear. The boundary line is described as follows: Starting at Pearse Canal and following the Canadian-Alaskan boundary northwesterly to Mt. St. Elias on the 141-degree meridian; thence north along the Canadian-Alaskan boundary to Mt. Natazhat; thence north along the divide of the Mentasta Range to Mt. Mentasta Pass; thence in a general westerly direction along the divide of the Alaska Range to Houston Pass; thence westerly following the 62nd parallel of latitude to the Bering Sea.

Polar bear must be taken either in U.S. or Canadian-held water or land mass in order to be eligible. However, the record book is

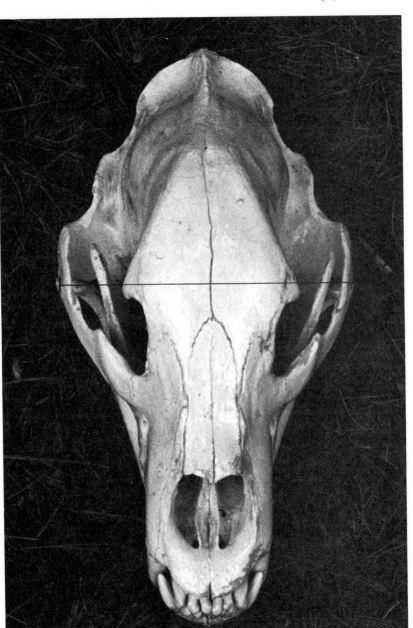

Also included in the measurement is the width of the skull from its two widest points.

Because of the Marine Mammal Protection Act, the record book is closed to new polar bear entries. The Protection Act prohibits polar bear hunting in Alaska and prohibits U.S. citizens who have taken a polar bear elsewhere from bringing the hide into the U.S.

closed to new polar bear entries at this time because of the Marine Mammal Protection Act.

Minimum scores for entering trophy bear into the Boone & Crockett all-time record book are: brown bear—28; grizzly bear—24; and polar bear—27. At this writing, the record for each bear is as follows: brown—$30^{12}/_{16}$, taken on Kodiak Island, Alaska; grizzly—$27^{2}/_{16}$, taken on Dean River, British Columbia; polar—$29^{15}/_{16}$, taken near Kotzebue, Alaska.

North American Hunting Club

The North American Hunting Club has an annual hunter recognition program for which members send in a photo, Boone & Crockett score and details of their trophy hunt. Entries are judged, not on a minimum score, but on the size of the game animal as compared to the other entries from members.

Recognition is given for each species taken in four categories: bow, rifle, handgun and muzzleloader.

The NAHC President's Trophy is given to the member whom a panel of judges considers had the most challenging hunt. It may not be the largest animal. The hunt is judged based on quality and difficulty of the hunting experience.

Pope & Young

The Pope & Young Club is the official record-keeping organization for trophies taken by bowhunters. The Pope & Young Club uses the same scoring system as Boone & Crockett, with lower minimum entrance levels for each game species in consideration of the added difficulty in taking an exceptional animal by bow. Like Boone & Crockett, Pope & Young has trained official measurers throughout North America. Trophies that score high enough may be entered in both the Pope & Young Club and Boone & Crockett Club record books.

Minimum scores for inclusion in the Pope & Young book are: grizzly—19; polar—20; brown—20. At this writing, the number one bear are: grizzly—$25^{6}/_{16}$, taken along the Anzac River in British Columbia; polar—$26^{6}/_{16}$, taken on Cape Lisberne in Alaska; brown—$28^{7}/_{16}$, taken on Unimak Island in Alaska.

As I was completing this book, I received notice of an unofficial new number one grizzly. By the time you read this, it will probably be the official number one Pope & Young Club grizzly.

The big grizzly was taken by Derril Lamb, a bowhunter who lives in Brunswick, Maine. Lamb was scheduled to hunt grizzlies in May of 1986 with British Columbia guide John Blackwell, but a heart attack canceled his plans. By 1987, Lamb had recovered and was able to reschedule his hunt.

Hunting in the area of Moose Lake, British Columbia, Lamb and Blackwell were using tree stands along creeks where grizzlies were feeding on spawning suckers. After several days of hunting, Lamb shot, at 22 yards, a huge grizzly which traveled only 65 yards after being shot completely through the center of the lungs with an arrow. The skull measures 25^{13}/$_{16}$ inches, surpassing the official Pope & Young record grizzly by ^{7}/$_{16}$ of an inch and rating a listing in the top 30 grizzlies of all time in the Boone & Crockett records. Lamb's unfortunate heart attack put him at the right place at the right time to take a trophy of a lifetime.

Longhunter Society

The newest of the major big game records programs was established by the National Muzzle Loading Rifle Association. Designed to recognize trophies taken by muzzleloading hunters, it is called the Longhunter Society. The name ''Longhunter'' was chosen to honor those hunters/explorers who pushed across the Appalachian Mountains into the vast, unexplored land we now call Kentucky and Tennessee. Often alone, occasionally in small groups, they penetrated a virtually unknown wilderness. The name ''Longhunter'' was appropriate, for their journeys often lasted more than a year and were punctuated by solitude, hostile Indians, shelter under overhanging rocks and eating only what the land provided.

The Longhunter Society also follows the Boone & Crockett method of scoring big game trophies. The trophy must be taken with a muzzleloading firearm and rules of fair chase followed.

Since this is a new program as this book is being written, there are no bear entries. That means this record book is open for those muzzleloading rifle hunters who would like to get into the record book.

Minimum scores for bear to be listed in the record book are: grizzly—19; brown—21; and polar—22.

Safari Club International

The Safari Club International offers its members a trophy recognition program which includes a record book. Their scoring

To estimate the size of a bear, measure the distance across the pad of one of the bear's front feet in the tracks. Add to that one inch, and the measurement in inches is generally equal to the feet the bear's hide will square.

method on bear is the same as the Boone & Crockett Club. Minimum scores for inclusion are: grizzly—22; brown—25; and polar—26.

Safari Club International has designated brown and grizzly bear territories as follows: Bear taken within 75 miles of tidewater south of Nome are classed as Alaska brown bear. Bear taken more than 75 miles from tidewater south of Nome, and taken North of Nome, are classed as grizzly bear.

NRA Big Game Hunter Awards

The National Rifle Association has a big game hunter awards program for trophies taken by its members. The program breaks each North American species into four different categories: modern firearm—handgun; modern firearm—long gun; muzzleloading firearm; and bow and arrow.

Scoring for bear follows the Boone & Crockett Club method. The minimum score for both grizzly and brown bear is 18 inches. There is no award at this time for polar bear.

A Leatherstocking Award is awarded each year to NRA members taking any of the 29 categories of North American big game that meet the minimum standards. A statuette award for each hunt method specified for Big Game Hunter Awards has been patterned after a fictional character in James Fenimore Cooper's writing, *Leatherstocking Tales*. At the NRA annual meetings, Leatherstocking Awards for animals taken in the preceding calendar year are presented, providing there are entries meeting all stated requirements. The recipients of these awards are selected based on highest relative standing in *Records of North American Big Game* published by the Boone & Crockett Club.

The minimum score for grizzlies is 24 inches, and for brown bear 28 inches.

13

Preserving
Your Trophy Bear

A while back I was in a taxidermy shop when the owner had to break the news to a hunter that his guide hadn't taken proper care of his brown bear skin and that it was ruined. I thought I was going to see a grown man cry. He had invested $11,500 in his hunting trip, not to mention two years' worth of vacation time he had saved up for the hunt, and now all he had was a skull and a few pictures that weren't very good.

For many hunters, a big bear is a once-in-a-lifetime trophy that is taken at great expense in time, money and effort. It behooves them to know something about the proper way a bear skin should be preserved in the field.

The first step to take in making sure you will get a good trophy mount is to select the best taxidermist you can *before* you leave for your hunt. Find a taxidermist who frequently works with big bear. Look at samples of his bear mounts and examine them for small details. Pay close attention to the work around the eyes and ears. Look for small splits or unnatural appearances. Examine the work around the mouth and feet. Ask your prospective taxidermist for references, some who have bear mounts that are several years old. Go see those mounts and find out if the owners are happy with his work.

Don't expect a good taxidermist to be cheap. He is a skilled artist and craftsman, and as with most things in life, you get what

Be sure to check the work of your prospective taxidermist. Here, taxidermist Joel Stone points out the detailed work in this mount. Notice the base of the mount, which simulates the stream's edge where the bear was shot.

you pay for. At this writing, a full body mount on a big bear will cost from $1,500 to $3,000, and bear rugs are priced between $75 and $100 per running foot.

Once you select a taxidermist, let him or her know your bear hunt plans and desires for a trophy mount. He can be helpful as you decide how you want your bear mounted. With this decided, be sure you get from the taxidermist any special instructions he has for you to use on your hunt. For instance, many taxidermists who are going to do a full body mount on big bear want measurements taken of the bear before he is skinned. They may want measurements from the tip of the nose to the root of the tail, the height at the shoulders, circumference of the body behind the front legs and in the middle of the body, circumference of the neck and other measurements.

Also, ask your taxidermist about field care and shipping the skin and hide back to him. A good taxidermist can be a big help in planning your trophy care.

Bud Jones is a Georgia taxidermist who has mounted many big bear. He says that most guides are reliable and know how to properly handle bear skins, but often a new guide or one who gets in a big hurry will do a poor job of skinning, fleshing and salting.

A good fleshing job is a mark of an experienced guide. For the taxidermist to provide you with an attractive mount or rug, you must provide him with an extremely clean, well-fleshed hide.

Then the hunter winds up with a ruined trophy. During one spring Jones got three beautiful bear skins from one guide who didn't turn the ears when he salted the skins, and all of the hair fell off the ears.

I talked with another well-known bear taxidermist, Joel Stone, who said he had seen the same problems. Stone said that due to the fat content in a bear, its hair will slip faster after death than that of any other animal. The hair is released from the skin due to the action of bacteria which start growing as soon as the bear dies. The moister and warmer the skin, the faster the hair slips. For this reason, a bear should be skinned as quickly as possible after the pictures and any necessary measurements have been taken.

Both taxidermists told me that the hunter should be sure there is plenty of salt in the bear camp. If there is any doubt, the hunter should take 50 to 100 pounds of salt per bear. I have to agree with this, as I have been on several hunts when the guide ran out of salt due to poor planning, rain got into the bags of salt, more animals than expected were taken or a trip back for supplies didn't take place for some reason. A few dollars for extra salt is good insurance for your trophy.

Common table salt is the best type. The finer the salt the better, as fine grains can be rubbed into tight places that rock salt or ice cream salt can't. Some guides use the coarser types, and I make it a point to find this out before I go on my hunt. If they do use coarse salt, I offer to pay the price of their having fine salt for my skins.

Since most bear are to be made into rugs or mounted life-size, the skinning procedure is the same. With the bear on its back, a cut is made in the skin from the center of the throat to the end of the tail. From this line, cut down each leg all the way to the pad. Some bear skinners want to cut the pads off, but you should insist that they don't, especially if the bear is to be mounted life-size. Skin out the feet to the last joints, leaving the claws attached to the hide. The remainder of the job is to remove the skin from the carcass with a sharp knife, leaving as much fat and tissue on the carcass as possible. A good job of skinning can save a lot of work fleshing.

When the bear is skinned, the next step is for all fat and tissue to be fleshed from the skin. A good fleshing job is the mark of a good guide. The ears should be turned, the lips and nose should be split, and the pads should be left on but fleshed on the inside. This is so that salt can be hand-rubbed into all of these areas.

According to the taxidermists I talked to, a few guides will

Once your bear skin has been fleshed, do not wash it in water or a brine solution. Water and moisture are a skin's worst enemy.

You can't use too much salt on a fresh bear pelt. Make sure it gets into every crack and crevice. The salt will pull out the moisture in which bacteria thrive.

want to wash a bear skin in water or a brine solution. This should be avoided, as water and moisture are a skin's worst enemy. Don't worry about any mud and dirt in the hair; your taxidermist can take care of that when he gets the skin.

Once the fleshing is complete, salt should be rubbed over all the inside of the skin. Use a lot of salt. You can't use too much, and not using enough will ruin your skin. Make sure it gets into every crack and crevice. All bullet holes should be well salted. Salt pulls out all the moisture in which the bacteria thrive, so your goal is to completely dry the skin by using salt.

A mistake many hunters make when all of this is going on is

After being salted, bear skins should be stretched and hung to allow drainage of moisture away from the skin.

celebrating success by the fire rather than watching to make sure their guide or his helper is doing a thorough job of fleshing and salting the skin. This is not the time to turn your back on your trophy. On more hunts than I care to talk about I have had to get involved in the salting process in order to get a good coat of salt on the skin.

As a side note, packing out a fresh grizzly or brown bear skin that may weigh from 80 to 150 pounds is no easy task. This, along with caring properly for the skin, should earn your guide a healthy tip.

Once a heavy coat of salt is placed on the skin, it is best to hang the skin up, stretched out, so that the moisture being drained from the skin can run off. Be sure the freshly salted skin is not exposed to the sun, a camp stove or campfire. Keep it cool and in the shade. Be sure animals such as porcupines can't get to the skin; they like salt.

One day later, the guide should remove the salt, then resalt the skin, taking the same care to get clean salt into every crack and

NAHC member David Hofius, of Cortland, Ohio, with his impressive Alaskan brown bear. David shot the bear with a .54 caliber muzzleloader.

crease. Watch for folds or wrinkles in the skin, as they are often overlooked when salting, and this can result in hair slipping. Be sure all the edges of the skin are well-salted.

While the skin is being salted, the bear skull should have all the meat cut off and then it should be boiled in water to remove the remaining tissue. Once the skull is tissue-free and is removed from the hot water, a wire hook made from a coat hanger or a green stick should be used to pull the remaining brain tissue out through the opening where the spine joined the skull.

If you should kill a bear in the last day or two of your hunt so that there is not adequate time to go through these steps while you are there, talk to your guide about completing the salting and drying process after you are gone and shipping the pelt to you.

Two of the best guides I've seen at taking care of bear skins are Cy Ford and his son Spencer. They do a good job of fleshing as they skin a bear. When my wife and I hunt with the Fords, they let my wife help skin, but they make me stand back and shoot pictures. Cy claims I leave too much fat and tissue on the skin. While the Fords spend the next day working on the skin, I clean the skull. It gives me something to do and saves time so that we can get hunting again faster.

When it is time to return home, you should have a burlap bag, or as Joel Stone recommends, an army surplus canvas duffel bag in which to pack your dried bear skin. Since it should be dry, there is no need to pack it in anything waterproof, such as a plastic garbage bag, as this can cause heat to build up and start bacterial action again.

Keep your bear tag and any other necessary paperwork with your bear skin. While there are no restrictions on traveling with grizzly or brown bear skins, you should be able to prove it is a legal harvest at any time the skin is en route. As has been pointed out earlier in this book, you can't bring a polar bear skin into the United States.

Once you get home, get your bear skin to your taxidermist at once; don't put it off. If you have to ship it to him, call to let him know it's on the way and when it will arrive. I always put my bear skins in a freezer if there is any delay while traveling home or getting the skin to my taxidermist.

I have stored bear skins in freezers at airports where an overnight stop was necessary. Just tell an airline representative what you need and he will usually point you in the right direction. I have stored skins in hotel freezers and once talked a restaurant in

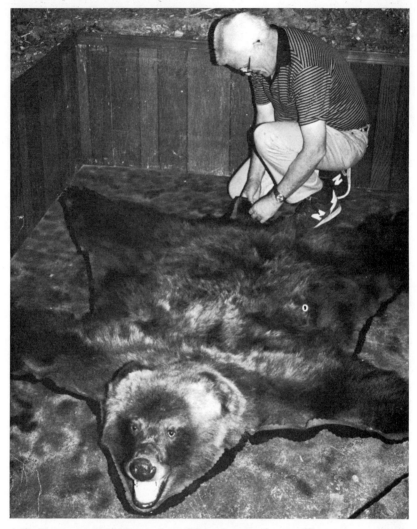

A big bear rug can be that perfect addition to your den or office.

Vancouver, British Columbia into letting me put a grizzly skin and skull in their freezer. I got some strange looks, but they agreed to it at no cost.

When the big day finally arrives and you get a call from your taxidermist to pick up your trophy, ask him for information on care and cleaning of the trophy. With proper care and an occasional cleaning, it should be in your trophy room for the rest of your life.

14

Big Bear
As Tablefare

Bear meat is wasted more than the meat from any other game animal in North America. The reason for this is the common belief that bear meat is "not fitten" to eat. It's a good thing the first European explorers in North America didn't have this hangup about eating grizzly meat, or many of them would have starved to death. Henry Kelsey, the first explorer to write about the big bear, first wrote in 1697 of how good the fierce and brutish bear were to eat.

Today, it is mostly natives of the Far North who save the meat from a fallen bear, and few sportsmen. I think if more would handle it with care and give it a try, they would find it much better tasting than they expected. I know I have.

Bear meat is as nutritious and as high in protein as domestic meat, but the flavor is entirely different. It varies with what food the bear has eaten. If the bear has been eating a steady diet of berries, he will be much more tasty than one which has been eating fish or moose carrion. In many areas, mid- to late-fall and early-spring grizzlies are usually tastier. Fall bear fill up on berries before denning, and spring bear feed on over-wintered cranberries uncovered by melting snow.

Another factor that determines how good a bear is to eat is its age. Young bear are always more tender and better tasting than old bear.

One year I had a group of four hunters who were very picky about the camp food, insisting that they didn't want any wild game served in camp. When one of the hunters got a grizzly on a moose kill, he and his partner sat a distance away reveling in the success of their hunt as I skinned the bear. I cut the loins out of the fat bear and slipped them into a plastic bag and put them in my jacket. When we arrived back at base camp, the cook made a big pot of stew from the bear meat. That night those four hunters cleaned the big stew pot and asked for more. They bragged about that meal a year later when I saw them at a sportsman's show near their home. To this day, they think they were eating beef. It goes to show that much of what we think about eating bear meat is in our minds, not our taste buds.

The first rule for having tasty bear meat is to try to kill the animal as quickly as possible. Any animal that is wounded and must be followed and shot again has adrenalin flowing, and the meat will not be as good.

Next, the bear should be skinned as quickly and cleanly as possible. When skinning a bear, be careful not to touch the hair with your hand or knife and then the meat. The hair contains a strong oil that will taint the meat. As soon as possible, the meat should be boned out and hung in cheesecloth sacks to cool down. An average grizzly will yield about 100 to 130 pounds of meat.

If the bear meat is to be frozen, it should be double-wrapped with butcher paper and marked with the name of the cut and the date it was wrapped. The date is important, as grizzly meat does not freeze well. Three months is the maximum length of time it should be frozen.

In the case of the polar bear, you should not keep the liver, as it has an extremely high concentration of Vitamin A and can be deadly.

All bear meat, like domestic pork, must be well-cooked to eliminate the threat of trichinosis. Home freezing does not make bear meat safe to eat without thorough cooking. Always use a meat thermometer. The meat will be safe when its internal temperature reaches 150 degrees F. Microwave cooking is not recommended because of uneven heating.

Never make jerky out of bear meat. The temperatures at which meat is dried into jerky are not high enough to kill trichinosis in the meat. Also, the high fat content in bear meat makes it susceptible to spoiling.

Almost any recipe that calls for pork can be used for bear. Bear

Generally, a bear that has eaten a steady diet of berries will be better tasting than one which has been eating fish and moose carrion. An average grizzly will yield about 100 to 130 pounds of meat.

that is tender may be cut into steaks and chops. If the people in your camp or home are worried about a "wild taste," you can rub the chops or steaks with lemon juice, powdered sweet marjoram and a few caraway seeds before cooking. Then top them with dill butter after cooking.

Another use for bear meat that eliminates any "gamey" taste is to grind it into hamburger (you may want to add a little beef suet) and use it in highly-seasoned recipes, such as chili and meat sauce for spaghetti.

Here are a few bear recipes you should try:

Bear Marinade
   2 cups vinegar
  12 whole cloves
   2 cups water
   1 tsp. allspice
 1-2 T. sugar
   3 medium-sized onions, sliced
   4 bay leaves
   1 tsp. salt

Cover the roast and refrigerate for at least 24 hours.

Bear Roast
   1 boneless roast, about 8 lbs.
 3-4 garlic cloves
   2 carrots, chopped
   1 stick of celery, chopped
   1 large onion, chopped

First marinate the roast as described above. Then insert slivers of garlic into the roast. Surround with vegetables and cook at 350 degrees F. until meat thermometer reads 150 degrees F., about 1½ hours.

Bear Steaks

½ cup flour
½ tsp. cloves
1 tsp. ginger
  bear steaks

Cut steaks one inch thick. Mix flour, cloves and ginger. Pound the mixture into the meat on both sides. Brown in vegetable oil in a moderately hot cast iron skillet. Salt and pepper after browning. Cover skillet and simmer 10 to 15 minutes. Always cook until well done.

Bear Stew

4 lbs. bear meat, cubed
1 cup fresh mushrooms, sliced
1 onion, chopped
1 garlic clove, diced
4 T. oil
1 cup beef broth or consomme
1 stick celery, chopped
1 10-ounce can tomato sauce
3 carrots, chopped
2 T. Worcestershire sauce
1 cup turnips, diced
3 medium potatoes, cubed
1 bay leaf
½ cup frozen peas

Flour meat and brown in oil. Add all ingredients except potatoes, peas and mushrooms and cook 1½ to 2 hours. Add the potatoes; cook for 20 minutes. Add mushrooms and peas and cook another five minutes. Drop dumplings by spoonful on top and cook, uncovered, for 10 minutes. Cover and cook 10 minutes longer.

Dumplings
1 cup flour
½ tsp. salt
2 T. butter
2 tsp. baking powder
1 egg, well beaten
½ cup milk

Sift all dry ingredients together, then stir in the butter, milk and egg and mix till moist. Use at once in stew.

Pickled Bear Paws
4 bear paws, skinned and washed
4 peppercorns
  water to cover
1 T. tarragon wine vinegar
1 onion, sliced
1 T. brown sugar
1 carrot, sliced
2 bay leaves
½ cup white vinegar
1 T. salt

Put the paws in a sauce pan and add the water, onion, carrots, vinegar, sugar, bay leaves, salt and peppercorns. Cook slowly until the gelatinous part of the paws is soft and the liquid has reduced to about one cup. Cool, cut the paws into pieces and place in a sterilized jar. The jelly that forms is delicious and should be served along with the meat.

Look for more bear recipes in *North American Hunter* and the *NAHC Wild Game Cookbook*. Don't form an opinion about bear meat until you have tried some. Chances are, if you get a berry-fed bear, you will have some good eating.

15

The Future
Of Big Bear Hunting

The polar, brown and grizzly bear are truly animals of the wilderness, and as man and his activities encroach on the rapidly-diminishing wild areas of North America, these bear pay the price. This has been seen dramatically in the lower 48 states.

When the first European explorers entered the western half of the U.S., they found grizzlies in parts of what has become 17 western states. It has been estimated that as many as 100,000 grizzlies called this area home. Truthfully, we have no way of determining an accurate number, but we do know that the population was substantial. In 1824, a Kentuckian named James Ohio Pattie led an expedition into the southwestern part of the country. During one day of travel along the Arkansas River, he recorded seeing 220 grizzlies.

Beginning with the early fur traders, bear numbers declined where man and bear lived in the same area. This decline was partly due to the indiscriminate killing of the big animals as pests. However, other factors played a major role in this decline, including loss of habitat to farms and ranches, reduction of prey, mining, timber cutting, railroad construction and predator control.

The grizzly had disappeared from the west coast beaches by the 1870s, the prairie river bottoms in the 1880s, open mountain valleys by 1899 and most foothill country by 1915. Grizzlies were last seen in Texas in 1890, North Dakota in 1897, California in

Big bear are truly animals of the wilderness.

1922, Utah in 1923, Oregon and New Mexico in 1931, Arizona in 1935 and Colorado in 1979. Grizzlies, retreating from the urbanization of the West, are now found in only six areas, within which there remain fewer than 1,000.

The best known of these grizzly environments, or ecosystems, is the Yellowstone. This area includes Yellowstone National Park, Grand Teton National Park and five surrounding national forests, for a total of four million acres. It has been estimated that 250 to 350 grizzlies remain in the area.

The Northern Continental Divide ecosystem encompasses Glacier National Park and the wilderness areas and associated lands south to the Blackfoot drainage and northwest to the Kootenai drainage. This is the only remaining place in the lower 48 states where the grizzly can be legally hunted. It is difficult to estimate bear numbers in this area, as it joins Canada's Waterton National Park and vast forest lands in Alberta and British Columbia. Hunting opportunities for grizzlies in Montana are very limited.

The Cabinet Yaak ecosystem contains some 1,800 square miles

in the northwest corner of Montana. It is estimated that only about 25 grizzlies are in that area.

On the Montana-Idaho line is the Bitterroot-Selway ecosystem, which is in part of the country's largest mountainous wilderness below Alaska. This ecosystem is in the Bitterroot Mountains and associated wilderness lands north to the Salmon River and west to the Selway drainage in northcentral Idaho. It is not known how many grizzlies live in this vast area.

The Selkirk Mountains ecosystem is located in the Selkirk Mountains in northeast Washington and the panhandle of Idaho. Between 12 and 40 grizzlies live in that ecosystem.

In western Washington is the North Cascades ecosystem, located in the northern edge of the Cascade Mountains. Few grizzlies remain in this scenic country.

The outlook for grizzly hunting in the lower 48 is not bright for the foreseeable future. Most ecosystems simply do not have huntable populations. Some of the most populous areas are within national parks, and, of course, no hunting is allowed there. In fact, at this writing, the National Park Service would like to eliminate all human activity in the bear's principal areas during periods when they are not hibernating.

Montana will continue to have a limited grizzly season as long as the population, most importantly the productive female population, can withstand some hunting pressure.

It has taken a long time for funds to become available and wildlife management techniques to be developed to conduct in-depth bear studies and management. This has now come about, and work is currently being done to help save the grizzly. This effort has an uphill battle yet to face, as so much is being done in the name of progress and recreation that is counter-productive to grizzly habitat and behavior. Those of us who want to hunt grizzlies will have to look north for the years ahead, keeping in mind that the same thing that has happened to the grizzly in the lower 48 could happen in Canada and Alaska as well.

Canadian Outlook

Fortunately, the big bear have fared much better in Canada than in the U.S. While habitat destruction and abuse of the grizzly have occurred in some locales, a lot of bear hunting is left. Thanks to the research and management practices followed by the various Canadian wildlife agencies, the grizzly is holding his own in many areas.

Best-known for big coastal grizzlies and many interior grizzlies is British Columbia. While the province doesn't have as large a number of bear in some areas as it once had, due to the influence of man's heavy hand, the population is estimated at 5,000 to 8,000 grizzlies. According to the game officials I talked to, the outlook is good for the future. Most of the guides in British Columbia have exclusive guiding rights to a specific area, and the ones I've hunted with do a good job of taking care of the bear in their area. Future generations of bear hunting and in turn their future income depend on it.

The Yukon has a grizzly population estimated at 5,000 animals, and the population seems to be stable. I am told that slightly more than half of the grizzly quota is being harvested, so this means a lot of mature bear are available. If the bear situation in the Yukon has a problem in the future, it is likely to be from mineral development. This activity is on the increase and is opening access to some remote areas. This could lead to a decline in grizzly numbers.

Alberta has had some trophy-class bear taken in the past, but like the lower 48, the province has seen some big changes in bear population. At the present, the grizzly population is estimated at 800 animals. Most of these bear are found along the western border, especially in the areas of Jasper and Banff National Parks. Grizzly hunting is now controlled through a limited entry draw available only to residents. In 1987, the grizzly harvest was 43. The outlook for non-residents in the future doesn't look good at this time.

The Northwest Territories is a vast land with few people, and because so much of it is uninhabited, any grizzly population estimate is just a guess. Several areas, primarily in the western and northwestern sections of the territory, do have huntable populations, and grizzly biologists there say the population appears to be stable.

This is one area that is looking up for grizzly hunters, as non-residents are now permitted to hunt in a few areas on a limited basis. While the harvest quota is not being increased, some native residents are giving up their own rights to hunt in order to guide sport hunters. As a growing number of natives look to this more lucrative use of their bear tags, hunting opportunities for non-residents will increase.

British Columbia holds one of the brightest futures for grizzlies, and Alaska's harvest continues at a healthy rate.

Alaskan Outlook

The brightest grizzly hunting outlook comes from Alaska. Alaska's brown/grizzly population is currently estimated at between 32,000 and 43,000 animals. Biologists' field reports show the Alaskan brown/grizzly bear populations continuing to appear healthy and abundant. The harvest for 1987 was 1,212 bear, a great increase over 1961 when only 471 bear were taken.

Alaska has a good bear management program, and prospects for the future, at least on the surface, appear to be very good. However, there are many factors beyond sport hunting and bear management that can and do have a major impact on brown/grizzly bear. The same factors which almost wiped out the grizzly in the lower 48 are at play in Alaska.

Livestock production, agriculture, mining, industrial expansion, urban expansion, homesteading, oil exploration, hydroelectric production and general road construction are all counterproductive to the well-being of big bear. Unrestricted hunting by native claims, bear/man confrontations by recreationists and defense-of-life-or-property kills will also play major roles in the future of the bear. Alaska is a state receiving much attention from all of these interests, and sportsmen, as well as wildlife planners, must be involved in the long-range planning for growth in this state if the bear situation is to remain as good as it is at present. We are fortunate that the state is still made up mostly of federal lands, which gives the sportsmen a say-so in planning; however, there is a potential danger built in, as public lands are managed by bureaucrats who are often more involved with the mechanics of politics than in doing a good job with sound planning for the future of wildlife management. A federal and/or state administration with strong leanings toward development of our federal lands could destroy the brown/grizzly populations in a relatively short period.

While we enjoy the good hunting in Alaska now, let's remember what happened to the big bear in the lower 48 and make sure the same thing doesn't occur in the 49th state.

Polar Bear Outlook

The polar bear in North America covers a vast range, extending from Newfoundland and James Bay northward 2,000 miles and laterally across the Arctic some 2,700 miles. This includes the northern coast of Alaska, the Yukon and Northwest Territories, as well as the provinces along the Hudson Bay.

The North American polar bear population is currently stable. Alaska may have an open season in the future.

With sound wildlife management and habitat control, future generations of NAHC members will be able to enjoy hunting big bear.

Until the enactment of the Marine Mammal Protection Act of 1972, Alaska offered excellent polar bear hunting to those who could afford the two ski-equipped planes usually used in this sport. It was very risky hunting, and more than one guide with hunter disappeared or got into serious trouble out on the ice pack.

It was not a declining population of polar bear in North America that brought about the Marine Mammal Protection Act of 1972. Instead, it was the unlimited hunting for hides in Russia that necessitated the act. As a result, all hunting of polar bear was stopped in Alaska except that done by native peoples, and they cannot sell the hides. At this writing, the only polar bear hunting available in North America is that offered by the native villages in northern Canada. Hunts there must be conducted by dogsled, and the hides cannot be brought into the U.S. The hunts are expensive and extremely demanding, both physically and mentally.

The polar bear population in North America is at a healthy number, according to wildlife biologists. The number is impossible to determine, as these animals range far and wide. The worldwide population has been estimated at 15,000. Currently, the annual harvest in North America is about 600, with the vast majority of those taken by natives for food, clothing and dog food. A few are killed around oil drilling camps and other populated areas as self-protection.

The future of hunting polar bear remains uncertain. Several hunting organizations are working toward getting Alaska opened back up for sport hunting, since it is well established that the bear population could withstand regulated hunting pressure. These organizations are also working for changes to allow Canadian hides to be brought into the U.S. by sport hunters.

While the North American polar bear population seems secure at this time, many factors will determine its numbers in the future. Since the polar bear diet is comprised mainly of seals, any decline in the seal population affects the bear population. During recent years, there has been some decline in seal numbers, and as I worked on this book, a virus was killing large numbers of seals in the North Sea. Another factor which could affect the polar bear is climatic change, such as a warming trend in the Arctic. And, the threat from water pollution becomes more serious every year.

Like the environment of all big bear, the polar bear's habitat must be watched carefully. However, at present there is a huntable polar bear population, and perhaps when this book is updated, it will include polar bear hunting throughout the North American Arctic.

Overall Outlook

The future of all the big bear rests in the hands of man. If we are to continue to have huntable populations, certain concessions must be made by land managers, developers, public land administrators, politicians and everyone else who affects bear habitat. We are fortunate to have the number of big bear we have, and, unfortunately, we probably can't expect to see much increase in these numbers in the future.

However, we hunters can do much toward keeping the big bear at their current level. We can suggest land use that favors the protection of the bear and its habitat. We can support sound wildlife management research and practices that affect the bear and its future. We can get involved with our politicians in the decision-making process that determines what happens on public lands. We can learn more about habitat and seclusion needs of the big bear and let our elected officials know we support big bear management as opposed to mining, timber cutting, road building and other development.

Most importantly, we must make sure our own attitudes are conducive to the conservation of big bear. Our first goal must be to preserve grizzly, brown and polar bear in their natural habitat. To have huntable populations is a bonus. Hunting is secondary to conservation and with any species, it is irresponsible to hunt it at the expense of over-kill.

With support from citizens, good wildlife management and

Atcheson & Son's, Inc.
3210 Ottawa St.
Butte, Montana 59701

Bar X Ranch
Nabesna Road
Gakona, Alaska 99586

Big River Hunting & Trapping
Bob Hannon
P.O. Box 22
Koyuk, Alaska 99753
(907) 963-3221

Canoe Bay Outfitters
P.O. Box 187
Sand Point, Alaska 99661
(907) 383-3844

Cox, Dick
P.O. Box 36
Yakutat, Alaska 99689

Farmen, Darrell
1200 E. 76th Ave., Suite 1228
Anchorage, Alaska 99518
(907) 344-9719

Feje's Guide Service, Ltd.
P.O. Box 111394
Anchorage, Alaska 99511
(907) 349-4040

Fitzgerald, Kevin
P.O. Box 375
Talkeetna, Alaska 99676
(907) 733-2704

Frost Guide Service
P.O. Box 112449
Anchorage, Alaska 99511
(907) 345-2862

Grizzly Skins of Alaska
P.O. Box 876-110
Wasilla, Alaska 99710

Gunlogson, Dick
P.O. Box 193
Willow, Alaska 99688
(907) 495-6434

Guthrie, Richard A.
P.O. Box 24-0163
Anchorage, Alaska 99524
(907) 243-7766

Hancock, John
P.O. Box 481
Kodiak, Alaska 99615
(907) 486-5644

Heinz Guide Service
3000 Porcupine Tr.
Anchorage, Alaska 99516
(907) 345-0908

Hersher, Rick
P.O. Box 140376
Anchorage, Alaska 99514
(907) 279-9874

Jake's Alaskan Wilderness Outfitters
P.O. Box 104179
Anchorage, Alaska 99517
(907) 248-0509

Keeline, Jim
P.O. Box 1333
Juneau, Alaska 99801
(907) 586-2827

Kichatna Guide Service
P.O. Box 670790
Chugiak, Alaska 99567
(907) 696-3256

Lane, Karl E.
P.O. Box 295
Juneau, Alaska 99802
(907) 586-3822

Matfay, Larry
Box 2
Old Harbor, Alaska 99643

Mountain Enterprises Guide Service
Tom Rigden & Brad Langvardt
P.O. Box 4127
Soldotna, Alaska 99669
(907) 262-3991

Munsey's Brown Bear Camp
Amook Pass
Kodiak, Alaska 99615
(907) 847-2203

North American Outfitters
Box 40015
Clear, Alaska 99704
(907) 582-2354

Pinnell & Talifson
Olga Bay
Kodiak, Alaska 99615

Pioneer Outfitters
Chisana, Alaska 99566
(907) 822-3306

Rivers, Larry
P.O. Box 107
Talkeetna, Alaska 99676
(907) 733-2473

Rohrer's Bear Camp
Box 2219
Kodiak, Alaska 99615
(907) 486-5835

Sheep River Camps
H.C.R. 3, Box 8449-A
Palmer, Alaska 99645

Smith, Jack
P.O. Box 1
McGrath, Alaska 99627
(907) 524-3274

Smith, T.F.
3407 HPR
Sitka, Alaska 99835
(907) 747-8807

Spiridon Bear Camp
Box 483
Kodiak, Alaska 99615
(907) 486-5436

Vrem, Kelly
P.O. Box 640742
Chugiak, Alaska 99567
(907) 892-7999

Vrem, Tracy
P.O. Box 130
Chugiak, Alaska 99567
(907) 688-2419

Warren, "Curly" M.J.
P.O. Box 670577
Chugiak, Alaska 99567
(907) 688-2187

Westwind Guide Service
P.O. Box 771224
Eagle River, Alaska 99577
(907) 694-2047

Wirschem, Chuck
6608 Blackberry
Anchorage, Alaska 99502
(907) 243-1649

Woods Outfitting
P.O. Box 827
Palmer, Alaska 99645

Montana
A Lazy H Outfitters
P.O. Box 729
Choteau, Montana 59422
(406) 466-5564

Pine Hills Outfitters
Mike Barthelmess
P.O. Box 282
Lincoln, Montana 59639
(406) 362-4664

Alberta
Silvertip Outfitters
Box 515
Midnapore, AB T0L 1J0
(403) 256-5018

British Columbia
Big Bear Guides & Outfitters
P.O. Box 1842
British Columbia V0J 3G0
(616) 782-2675

Bucking Horse & Besa River Outfitters
P.O. Box 6884
Fort St. John, BC V1J 4J8
(604) 773-6468

Christina Falls Outfitters, Inc.
Darwin Watson
Box 6640
Fort St. John, BC V1J 4J1
(604) 787-9624

Collingwood Brothers Guides & Outfitters
Box 3070
Smithers, BC V0J 2N0
(604) 847-9692

Dorsey, Dave
P.O. Box 3472
Anahim Lake, BC V0L 1C0
(604) 742-3251

Finlay River Outfitters
RR 4, Site 19, Camp 12N
Prince George, BC V2N 2J2
(604) 562-7826

Folding Mtn. Outfitters Ltd.
P.O. Box 304
Stavely, AB T0L 1Z0
(403) 549-3856

Granby Guides & Outfitters
RR 1
Grand Forks, BC V0H 1H0
(604) 442-2849

Innes Marine Charters
RR 1, Box 9
Campbell River, BC V9W 3S4
(604) 923-6512

Kawdy Outfitter
General Delivery
Smither, BC V0J 2N0

Love Bros & Lee
RR 1, Kispoix Rd
Hazelton, BC V0J 1Y0
(604) 842-6350

Mitchell-Cross Outfitters
Box 111
Edgewater, BC V0A 1E0

Muskwa Safaris Ltd.
Box 6488
Fort St. John, BC V1J 4H9
(604) 785-4681

One Eye Outfit
P.O. Box 4045
Williams Lake, BC V2G 2V2
(604) 398-8329

Palliser River Guides & Outfit
Box 238
Radium, BC V0A 1M0
(604)347-9274

Redfern Guiding Services
Cy Ford
P.O. Box 492
Fort St. James, BC V0J 1P0
(604) 996-8410

Ross, R. Lynn
Pink Mountain, BC V0C 2B0
(604) 787-7245

Skeena Mtn. Outfitters
6821 Lilac Crescent
Prince George, BC V2K 3H2
(604) 962-7995

Steciw, Igor
P.O. Box 2665
Smithers, BC V0J 2N0
(604) 847-3055

Tahaltan Outfitters
General Delivery
Telegraph Creek, BC V0J 2W0
(604) 235-3401

Taku Safari, Inc.
Box 268
Atlin, BC V0W 1A0
(604) 746-5322

Upper Stikine River Adventures
RR 1 Boundry Rd.
Telkwa, BC V0J 2X0
(604) 846-5001

Vents River Safaris
P.O. Box 37
Moncho Lake, BC J0C 12O

Yohetta Wilderness, Ltd
P.O. Box 69
Duncan, BC V9L 3X1

Ontario
Canada North Outfitting
Jerome Knap
P.O. Box 1230
Waterdown, ON L0R 2H0
(416) 689-7925

Yukon Territories

Ceaser Lake Outfitters
P.O. Box 484
Watson Lake, YT Y0A 1C0
(403) 536-2174

Dickson Outfitters
708 Minto Rd Crestview
Whitehorse, YT Y1A 3X9

Jensen, Peter Guide & Outfitter
58 Alsek Rd.
Whitehorse, YT Y1A 3K4
(403) 667-2030

Kusawa Outfitters
28 Alsek Rd.
Whitehorse, YT Y1A 3K2
(403) 667-2755

Low, Doug/Outfitter
General Delivery
Tagish, YT Y0B 1T0
(403) 399-3171

McMillan River Outfitters
P.O. Box 5088
Whitehorse, YT Y1A 4S3

Ostashek Outfitting Ltd.
Box 4146
Whitehorse, YT Y1A 3S6
(403) 668-7323

Pelly Mountain Outfitters
P.O. Box 4492
Whitehorse, YT Y1A 2R8
(403) 633-6606

Young, Dave/Outfitters Ltd.
Site 12 Comp 24, RR. 1
Whitehorse, YT Y1A 4Z6
(403) 668-4518

Yukon Outfitters
Box 5364
Whitehorse, YT Y1A 4Z2
(403) 667-2712

Appendix B:
Fish & Game Departments

When you begin to plan your big bear hunt, contact the fish and game department in the state or province that you intend to hunt. They can provide you with information about hunting regulations, nonresident licenses, big bear guides and outfitters, harvest trends and last-minute licensing or regulation changes.

Alaska
Department of Fish & Game
P.O. Box 3-2000
Juneau, Alaska 99802
(907) 465-4100

Montana
Fish, Wildlife & Parks
1420 E. 6th Avenue
Helena, Montana 59620
(406) 444-2950

Alberta
Fish & Wildlife Division
Main Floor., North Tower
Petroleum Plaza
9945-108 St.
Edmonton, Alberta T5K 2G6
(403) 427-6750

British Columbia
Ministry of the Environment
Parliament Building
Victoria, British Columbia V8V 1X4
(604) 387-9717

Northwest Territories
Department of Renewable Resources
Legislative Building
Yellowknife, N.W.T. X1A 2L9
(403) 920-8716

Yukon Territory
Fish & Wildlife
P.O. Box 2703
Whitehorse, Yukon Territory Y1A 2C6
(403) 920-8716

Appendix C:
Record Books &
Awards For Bear

Boone & Crockett Club
241 S. Fraley Blvd.
Dumfries, VA 22026
(703) 221-1888

Longhunter Society
P.O. Box 67
Friendship, IN 47021
(812) 667-5131

NRA, Hunter Services Division
1600 Rhode Island Avenue NW
Washington, D.C. 20036
(202) 828-6246

North American Hunting Club
P.O. Box 35557
Minneapolis, MN 55435
(612) 941-7654

Pope & Young Club
1804 Borah
Moscow, ID 83843
(208) 882-3084

Safari Club International
4800 W. Gates Pass Rd.
Tucson, AZ 85745
(602) 620-1220

Index

238